GW00726082

Today's Christian Kindergarten

Today's

TODAY'S CHRISTIAN KINDERGARTEN is the successor to *The Christian Kindergarten* which was published in 1953 and reprinted in 1959, and which has now been exten sively revised and rewritten. TODAY'S CHRISTIAN KINDERGARTEN is essentiall a new book that incorporates the latest developments in Christian kindergarte education

Christian Kindergarten

By Morella Mensing, M. A.

Supervising teacher of Grace Lutheran School, the campus
school of Concordia Teachers College, River Forest, Illinois;
also visiting assistant professor of education, Concordia
Teachers College; and part-time instructor at The National
College of Education — Urban Campus in Chicago, Illinois.

Concordia Publishing House   Saint Louis, Missouri

Library of Congress Catalog Card No. 75-174468
ISBN 0-570-01506-5

MANUFACTURED IN THE UNITED STATES OF AMERICA

Dedicated with affection —
To all little boys and girls,
of whom the Savior has said,
". . . of such is the kingdom of God."

PREFACE

A dreary place would be this earth
Were there no little people in it;
The song of life would lose its mirth
Were there no children to begin it.
— *Author Unknown*

Children are the most interesting creatures on earth. The more we know about them, the easier it is to get along with them and to be successful in teaching them. The more we realize that our Lord and Savior loved them and died and rose again for them, the more real joy we shall find in working with them.

This book is intended to provide help and guidance for teachers and others who are responsible for teaching and training young children, particularly those in Christian kindergartens. It deals with the nature and environment of the young child, and with techniques and procedures that make for successful kindergarten teaching.

The Christian kindergarten, in fact any kindergarten, is not a school, but exactly what its name implies, a garden—a place to grow. It is a place where children live for part of the day with others of their own age, under the Christian guidance of adults. It should by all means be a place where the Christian life is lived naturally, on the level of the four- and five-year-old child.

While a good kindergarten does not circumscribe the areas of learning too closely nor too rigidly, it does present plan and purpose. The program suggested in this book is flexible enough to meet the ever-changing demands in preschool education today. It may be adjusted to the intellectual maturity of some children, to the fleeting interests of others, and to the many birthday parties and holidays, which are natural and happy occasions in every kindergarten.

The child who comes to kindergarten brings his whole self with him. He comes as a total being with his whole self developing day after day. To be effective in training the young child, the program of study for the kindergarten must be as integrated as life itself. While accepting this developmental approach, one dare not overlook recent research supporting the young child's need for intellectual content. Plans and procedures will depend a great deal on the group to be taught, the environment, the rest of the school, and the homes and community; but harmonious Christian living and a natural integration of subject matter are to be ever present goals.

TODAY'S CHRISTIAN KINDERGARTEN is the outgrowth of many years of living with small children at work and play. The ideas and practices here presented do not represent the only way of doing things and handling given situations, but they have proved successful with little children over a period of years. Each year one gains new insights about young childrens' potential, so some of these new ideas are offered to you to try, to test, to use, to adapt, and to improve.

The material is intended to serve as a guide for teachers engaged in the education of young children. The book should serve as a ready reference for the beginning teacher who is planning her work and setting up her objectives; as an outline of procedure for the experienced teacher, who will be able to adapt it to her particular situation and modes of procedure; as a source of information for the student; and as a direct help for those who are too often thrown on their own resources when engaged to teach in a Christian kindergarten. It should find a welcome place in the library of the teachers-in-training, who will want to gain a mental picture of how and what children learn during their preschool years. It should help them understand the total-growth process of the children they will someday teach. To understand the older child, they will have to understand the younger. The child who is ten, once was five. The book may well serve also as a text for students in classes studying early childhood education.

While I assume full responsibility for the viewpoints and philosophy expressed throughout this book, I realize that my thinking has been influenced by many sources. So I wish to acknowledge my indebtedness to all who in one way or another have left their imprint on my thinking, either through the printed page or through personal association.

First, I wish to express my gratefulness for the Christian training I myself received from Christ-loving, understanding parents, and for the pleasant associations I had with my brothers and sister, all of whom made my own childhood a very happy one. At the same time I wish to thank my nieces and nephews and all the little boys and girls whom I have taught for the part they played in helping me understand more fully how little children live and learn.

I am also deeply indebted to my former associates, my present co-workers, and many good friends for some fine demonstrations of many of the principles embodied in this book, and for their devotion to the cause of Christian education. A heartfelt thanks goes to Mr. Frederick Nohl and Dr. Velma Schmidt for their impetus and encouragement in planning a revision; also to the many dedicated kindergarten teachers who in answering our questionnaires contributed new ideas and made valuable suggestions; to Mrs. Everet Lohman for her help on the religion adaptation; and to the teachers who let us visit in their classrooms. To you, Dr. William A. Kramer and Mr. David Rohde, comes a big "God bless you" for your outstanding work as my editors.

It is my prayer that the ultimate achievement of this book will be to lead little children to know God, to love Jesus, and to serve others.

Dear Jesus, bless each little child
And keep it in Thy care.
And bless the words within this book.
This is my fervent prayer.

THE AUTHOR

CONTENTS

Pictures and illustrations are the combined efforts of the author, Concordia Publishing House, family, and friends.

PART ONE

THE CHILD
AND THE KINDERGARTEN

1. The Purpose of a Christian Kindergarten

Dear Lord, I do not ask
That Thou shouldst give me some high
   work of Thine,
Some noble calling, or some wondrous
   task;
Give me a little hand to hold in mine;
Give me a little child to point the way
Over the strange, sweet path that leads
   to Thee;
Give me a little voice to teach to pray;
Give me two shining eyes Thy face to see.
The only crown I ask, dear Lord, to wear
Is this: That I may lead a little child.
I do not ask that I may ever stand
Among the wise, the worthy, or the great;
I only ask that softly, hand in hand,
A child and I may enter at the gate.
              — *Author Unknown*

CHILDREN ARE THE PROMISE
OF THE FUTURE

Children are the promise of the future. Economically and socially they are of tremendous importance to the nation, and the nation is aware of this fact. Many agencies are at work for the betterment of our youth. Pamphlets and books are at our service, newspapers carry articles on child training, and magazine articles dealing with child growth and development are appearing in increasing numbers.

An interest in children dates back as far as we have records. We know that in early Bible times children and their early education were held in high regard. Jewish fathers were earnestly admonished by God to teach and train their children diligently. The Greeks used early childhood to implant ideals and lay foundations for physical fitness. Rome emphasized child training. During the Middle Ages there were schools, and surely during the period of the Reformation education of the young child was impressed on parents as a Christian duty. Martin Luther refers again and again to the extreme importance of an early beginning in training "the tender plants," the small children.

Christ, more than anyone else, holds children in high esteem and shows His love and concern for them in His tender admonition: "Let the children come to me, do not hinder them; for to such belongs the kingdom of God" (Mark 10:14). The closer we approach His love for children, the better we will be able to help them grow in the faith and put their faith into action.

THE KINDERGARTEN

Comenius and John Locke were concerned about the education of infants and young children. Pestalozzi experimented with the education of young children. He pioneered in the use of psychology in education and continually emphasized that the child is more important than the subject. To Froebel, a student of Pestalozzi, we give the honor of starting the first kindergarten, in 1837, and for choosing a name so suitable, the "children's garden," that it has remained with us for over a hundred years.

In the United States the kindergarten idea was cordially received and greatly improved and extended. Kindergartens were started first in the German language and as private enterprises, and later in the English language with appropriations of public funds for their establishment and maintenance. The first kindergarten in the United States was established in 1856 at Watertown, Wisconsin, by Mrs. Carl Schurz, one of Froebel's pupils. Thus kindergarten was a school for German-speaking immigrants. The first distinctly American kindergarten was organized by Miss Elizabeth Peabody in Boston in 1860. St. Louis is given credit for first combining the kindergarten with the public school system. This was in 1873. Kindergartens were developed in the parochial schools somewhat later.

After 1880 the kindergarten movement had some ups and downs, but recently we have experienced a great revival of early childhood education. Educators today believe that the child's potential can either be "harnessed" or "harassed" at this tender age, thus greatly affecting future learning. Almost any book on education today emphasizes the importance of the "early years."

Noting the needs of young children in today's world, delegates to the 1960 White House Conference on Children and Youth placed great emphasis on nursery schools, day care centers, and kindergartens for fours and fives. The Headstart, Follow Up, and other projects of the War on Poverty, activated by the Office of Economic Opportunity, are evidences of this deep concern. Montessori Centers, so long a part of European education, which stress building of early learning patterns, are taking a prominent place in early education.

The education of young children ought to be the concern and challenge of any nation, but even more so of the church, which has a command for Christian education from God and a promise of His blessing. Being aware of the spiritual values of a Christian kindergarten, the church should answer its challenge, follow the command of Christ to "Feed My lambs," and establish Christian kindergartens in its midst.

THE CHURCH'S CHALLENGE

If the church wishes to meet its challenge in child training properly, it must offer a modern, efficient, and challenging program of preschool education to guide and direct the children during their most impressionable years.

Even though the little child today lives in a rapidly changing world, his experiences are not the same as those of his elders. Therefore it is important that an environment be provided for him in which he can live and learn with children of his own age group. The young child needs contact with other children to give his personality and character a chance

to develop under normal conditions, conditions conducive to his particular stage of development.

Besides being necessary, it is at the same time a pleasurable experience for a young child to learn to work and play with others and to be given practice in inhibiting some of his purely selfish tendencies and sinful instincts.

The Christian kindergarten is the answer to the educational and social needs of four- and five-year-olds. It recognizes the importance of the child's social growth together with proper physical and mental development. More than this, it recognizes the need for providing an environment that will foster both spiritual and moral growth in the little child and help him develop into a well-rounded, well-adjusted, Christian personality with an ever-increasing concern for others.

KINDERGARTEN CHILDREN PROFIT FROM INSTRUCTION

Children of kindergarten age can profit greatly from early guidance in Christian living and learning. Behavior patterns are becoming fixed at this time, and children are becoming aware of right and wrong. They are seeking answers to their little perplexities and are eager to please God and man. They are able to realize that they too are sinful and in need of salvation that is offered to them through Jesus Christ. They are happy to say:

> Jesus is my Savior,
> On the cross He gave
> His dear life a ransom
> Children, too, to save.

Although the child at this age has a limited capacity for learning facts, story details, and long memory verses or hymn verses, the teaching of simple religious truths is invaluable for building and establishing Christian habits, attitudes, ideals, and actions.

The child is also quick to reflect the general atmosphere of his surroundings, so it is important that the kindergarten be Christ-centered, with many opportunities for Christian living geared to the child's level.

FUNCTIONS OF THE CHRISTIAN KINDERGARTEN

Teaching Christian Truth and Christian Living. The Christian kindergarten encourages meaningful worship and a love for Holy Scripture through the medium of appropriate Bible stories, songs, memory gems, and purposeful activities. Through these various activities the child will be led to realize that God, the Creator, is still at work today and that human beings can have fellowship with Him and His dear Son, whom they will learn to love as their personal Savior from sin. Teaching the Christian faith and putting this faith into action will be the first and foremost aim of the Christian kindergarten.

Bridging the Gap Between Home and School. Another important function will be bridging the gap between the home and the school. A small child must step out of the home into a new and unfamiliar environment. An informal atmosphere saturated with a Christian understanding of and attitude toward little children will make it easier for

the small child to adjust slowly and happily to the formal school situation.

The child at this age is at the end of his rapid physical and mental growth. He is beginning to want to leave his home and parents occasionally. He wants to explore and venture out on his own. He can be away from his mother for short periods of time and is usually quite willing to become a member of a small group.

A Christian kindergarten is an ideal place for a child to make his entrance into the big world in which he is to live. The transition from home to school can be a happy one. Success here often has a great bearing on the intellectual and emotional life of the child throughout his school days. The efficient use of a child's intellectual powers is often affected by the stability of his emotional life. Thus the kindergarten will aim to stabilize the child emotionally by helping him to adjust slowly to situations that he will meet.

Preparation for Tomorrow. The best preparation for tomorrow is to live fully today. Therefore it is important that the kindergarten provide a stimulating environment for the preschool child with many direct

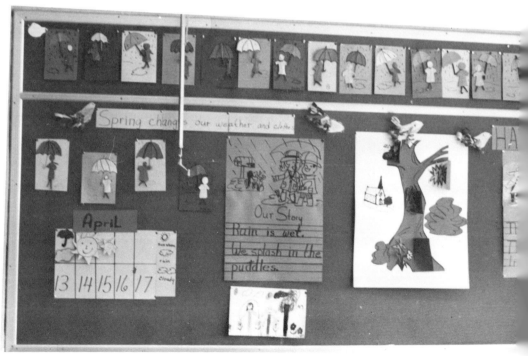

A SAMPLE RECORD BLANK

Name of Child _____

SPIRITUAL GROWTH

Enjoys the Bible stories
(1) Always   (2) At times   (3) Seldom

Shows signs of Christian behavior
(1) Marked   (2) Normal   (3) Very few

Participates in songs, memory gems, and activities
(1) Wholly   (2) At times   (3) Seldom

SOCIAL GROWTH

Respects the rights of others
(1) Fully   (2) At times   (3) Seldom

Plays with others
(1) Wholeheartedly (2) When urged   (3) Never

Is courteous
(1) Consistently   (2) When reminded (3) Never

Takes responsibility in seeing things through
(1) Completely   (2) At times   (3) Seldom

Is accepted by other children
(1) Completely   (2) At times   (3) Not at all

PHYSICAL GROWTH

Height _____ Weight _____ Speech _____

Eyes _____ Ears _____ Maturity _____

EMOTIONAL GROWTH

Displays a fair degree of confidence
(1) At all times   (2) Sometimes   (3) Never

Controls his feelings of anger
(1) At all times   (2) Fairly well   (3) Not yet

Keeps moods regular
(1) Yes   (2) No

Displays discouragement
(1) Often   (2) Sometimes   (3) Never

SKILLS

Is able to dress and undress
(1) Completely alone (2) With help   (3) Not at all

Moves about at his work
(1) With control   (2) Normally   (3) Awkwardly

Handles paints and tools
(1) Well   (2) Fairly well   (3) Poorly

Expresses himself through art creatively
(1) Skillfully   (2) Average   (3) Poorly

Carries a tune
(1) Well   (2) Average   (3) Not at all

Responds to rhythm
(1) Naturally   (2) Awkwardly   (3) Not at all

Uses language ability
(1) Remarkably   (2) Well   (3) Poorly

SOME SPECIAL INTERESTS

Remarks

Physical Play _____

Books and Stories _____

Music _____

Dramatic Play _____

Creative Art _____

REMARKS BY THE TEACHER

_____

_____

REMARKS BY THE PARENT

_____

_____

Date of Conference _____

A REPORT CARD

"My Kindergarten Progress Report," published by Concordia Publishing House, St. Louis, Missouri, offers a ready-made, four-page form for reporting a child's progress.

experiences for correct cognitive and conceptual learnings. Modern education concerns itself with the growth of the individual child and with the way he works and plays in a group, stressing the need for each child to live fully at every stage of development. The emphasis now in kindergarten is not on preparing the child for first grade or for formal education that may follow, but rather on helping him live a full and rich life as a maturing child.

This does not mean that the intellectual development of the child is ignored or neglected. On the contrary, it shows that educators and teachers have recognized the total growth process of children to be important and have learned the importance of a rich and varied content program that will challenge the young child of today.

A challenging program affords the child an opportunity to grow gradually and naturally in all areas of learning, without pressure or forcing. The value of this kind of training and learning does not lie in the increase of knowledge or facts, but rather in learning to work with others, to discover for himself, to solve problems, and to carry out some planned procedures.

If a kindergarten offers this kind of training, the children will be able to adjust more easily and happily to a challenging school environment and be assured of success in interpreting and understanding the complex world in which they live.

Building a Philosophy of Life. The kindergarten will also help the child build within himself a happy and secure philosophy of life. The religious and worship time, as well as the many quiet moments during the day, gives untold opportunities for teaching the faith and building a philosophy for living this faith. Under the guidance of the Holy Spirit, the Bible truths, the memory gems, songs, prayers, drama, and all available helps lead the child into communion with his Lord and Savior and into an acceptance of His love.

This Christian philosophy of life, which can be started in the child's formative years, will bring happiness to him and to those with whom he comes in contact, for it will reflect the love of Christ within him.

Training for Citizenship. The Christian kindergarten can also lay the foundation for a loyal, God-pleasing citizenship. The child can be taught the rightful meaning of his duty toward his country as a little citizen by participation in activities that are built around the country's heroes and special days. He can learn to love and honor his flag and to serve his country by being a faithful, obedient child in home and school, ever reflecting the faith that is in Him.

American Flag, I love you,
I love your colors true;
I love each star,
Each shining bar,
The red, the white, the blue.

COOPERATION WITH THE HOME

What is taught and practiced in the kindergarten must also be accepted in the home if there is to be a lasting effect or a permanent impression. The Christian kindergarten will try to bring about a close cooperation between the school and the children's homes.

The best teacher-parent contact can be made by direct visits in the homes. Here the teacher and the parents can observe the child in his natural surroundings under familiar conditions. A mutual confidence can be established between parents and teacher that will be invaluable.

Parent-teacher groups, mothers clubs, bulletins, and personal conferences with the parents all are means through which the home and school can be brought closer together. In these meetings problems of interest to all can be discussed and solutions offered. Parents should always be welcome visitors in the school.

CONFERENCES WITH THE PARENTS

The conferences in which the child's progress and general attitudes are discussed and evaluated with the parents are an excellent means of building a close, harmonious relationship between teacher, child, and parents. The building of this Christian relationship should be one of the prime functions of the kindergarten in a Christian school.

These conferences could be held several times during the school year—after school hours or in the evening. The type of report to be made will be determined somewhat by the policies of the school. An oral report to the parents is preferred. A written, informal report in the form of a letter may be sent at the end of the school year with a certificate of promotion.

A teacher will, after some experience, develop her own evaluation from which she can report the child's progress to the parent most effectively. (See page 17 for samples.)

A group meeting of all mothers is beneficial at the beginning of the school year so the parents may know what the kindergarten is trying to do for their children and so the teacher can become acquainted with the mothers personally.

WHAT THE CHRISTIAN KINDERGARTEN TRIES TO DO FOR THE CHILD

The Christian kindergarten leads the child to Christ, shows him his sin, but also reassures him of his Savior. It helps him live with his playmates in a God-pleasing manner, grow in social living, adjust to life outside the home as well as in school, and feel a secure and happy relationship between his parents and the school he attends. It offers him an education that is appropriate to his stage of development, satisfying to him at present, and preparing him for the years that are to follow, not merely in one phase of growth, but in his total growth process.

The following brief statements summarize what the Christian kindergarten should try to do for the child:

1. To lead the child to appreciate the wonders of God's creation and His great love in sending Jesus Christ as the Savior from sin.

2. To lead him to trust and believe in Jesus as his personal Savior from sin.

3. To teach the child to speak to God in prayer and to put his faith into action.

4. To help make his adjustment to school happy and wholesome.

5. To help the child become aware of, and have an interest in, the world about him.

6. To give each child many opportunities to work and play cooperatively in a group.

7. To teach the child to act and think for himself — to evaluate and make judgments.

8. To help the child feel at ease when talking to a group.

9. To give the child all kinds of experiences in a stimulating, challenging environment.

10. To help him develop desirable speech habits — to speak correctly and distinctly and to grow in vocabulary.

11. To teach him good sportsmanship — to be willing to lose at times.

12. To provide opportunities to work with all kinds of materials for fostering creative expression.

13. To follow the child's progress in all phases of growth through observation and through letters and conferences with parents.

14. To help the child feel a real sense of belonging and full acceptance with adults and with his peers.

15. To help him grow in the courtesies commensurate with his age.

16. To teach him how to live happily with and show concern for others.

17. To teach him to observe a few simple health and safety rules.

18. To help him develop love and tolerance for all people.

19. To develop in him a desire to tell others the story of Jesus and His love.

20. To help him manifest some degree of self-discipline and self-control.

21. To develop in him a sense of pride in his school, church, home, and community.

WHAT PARENTS CAN DO FOR THEIR CHILD

Parents will want to know how best to cooperate with the Christian kindergarten to achieve the purposes of Christian education and training. The following suggestions may help parents gain an insight into the goals and directives of a program of guiding the first steps in learning.

1. Make your child feel secure and wanted at all times.

2. Read and tell him stories about Jesus.

3. Teach him to pray, and pray with him.

4. Bring him early to the house of God.

5. Set a good example for him at all times.

6. Teach him to dress and undress himself.

7. Give him a place where he can hang up his wraps.

8. Give him a place where he can keep his playthings.

9. Take him into your conversations at the table.

10. Teach him his full name, his address, and his telephone number.

11. Teach him to appreciate his toys and to put them neatly away.

12. Sing songs with him and read good books to him.

13. Let him make things with his hands, using many kinds of media.

14. Take him regularly to the dentist and the doctor.

15. Show an interest in everything that he does.

16. Never make fun of the things he cannot do.

17. Do not threaten him with school or the teacher.

18. Try to keep regular eating and sleeping hours.

19. Teach him the way to and from school.

20. Let him share his toys with others.

21. Remind him to say "Please" and "Thank you," and teach him a few little courtesies in keeping with his development.

22. Study his growth pattern and expect progress accordingly—accept him where he is.

23. Do not make comparisons with other children in the family or in the neighborhood.

24. Teach the child to attend to his toilet needs without assistance.

25. Show him the use of cleansing tissue for a handkerchief and when coughing and sneezing.

26. Check carefully on immunization and vaccination.

27. Encourage questions and give correct answers.

28. Teach correct concepts and separate fact from fancy when possible.

29. Encourage him to experiment with and to create his own toys.

30. Help him express his feelings and aspirations.

31. Help him enjoy the spontaneous childhood experiences.

OTHER AREAS OF COOPERATION FOR PARENTS

There are other areas of parent cooperation besides good child training at home. Parents, for example, are largely responsible for the attitude their child takes toward the teacher and toward the kindergarten as such. Here are suggestions the teacher can make regarding the parents' part in achieving the purposes of the kindergarten. Parent-teacher meetings and private conferences offer opportunities for transmitting the suggestions to parents.

1. Make going to school a pleasurable experience—foster enthusiasm for learning.

2. Do not feel that you are a martyr when you send your child to school for the first time. Be proud to do so.

3. Send your child regularly and promptly.

4. Send a written excuse after each absence from school or call the teacher.

5. Tell the teacher anything about your child that will help her understand him better.

6. Be interested in what your child brings home from school. Never belittle it.

7. Listen to what he has to tell you. Do not coax him to tell things he does not wish to tell.

8. Put his name on his wraps and on his boots.

9. When you send money with him, place it in an envelope and write his name on the envelope.

10. Give him a good breakfast before he starts to school.

11. Come to school when he invites you for some special occasion.

12. If your child has a cold or symptoms of illness, keep him home from school.

13. Have complete confidence in your child's teacher, and let your child feel this strongly.

14. Never discuss the teacher, the playmates, the church, or the school negatively in the presence of your child.

15. If you have any questions, any misunderstandings, or any grievances, discuss these things with the teacher before telling others about them. As a rule difficulties can be ironed out quite easily when the approach is made in a Christian manner.

16. Show a deep interest in your child but not undue concern.

2. The Kindergarten Child

"But Jesus said, 'Let the children come to Me, and do not hinder them; for to such belongs the kingdom of heaven.'"
— Matthew 19:14

TEACHERS NEED TO UNDERSTAND CHILDREN

Everyone who is concerned with the Christian education of small children will want them to grow up well; to fit their own individual growth pattern; to have their own heritage of an abundant life; and, above all, to grow into useful citizens and noble sons and daughters of their Lord and Savior, Jesus Christ.

Teachers will be able to contribute more to the growth of children if they continually study them and through this study learn to understand them, their abilities, their potentialities, and their needs.

Christian teachers realize that children, even the best of them, are sinful beings, inclined to evil, but also the heirs and recipients of the full grace and love of God. They are redeemed by Christ and sanctified by the Holy Spirit.

Little children will have to be taught what is right and what is wrong. Much patience will have to be exercised by the teacher during the early period of learning, when many mistakes will be repeated, sometimes quite unconsciously and sometimes willfully. A teacher will have to learn to discriminate between deliberate sinful actions and mere forgetfulness, overexuberance, or immaturity by the child, and will have to deal with these accordingly.

The teacher who wishes to understand her children better will study Holy Scripture carefully to see what Christ Himself says of little children, how He feels toward them, and how He wants them to be taught and trained. Then she will avail herself of all the opportunities to read and to study child growth in its various aspects. She will also compare some "accepted" facts of child training with Scripture and choose those ways of dealing with the lambs of Christ that will make better adjusted, happier children, reared according to basic Christian principles. As her example she will take the Great Teacher of humanity, who, possessing a sympathetic understanding of childhood and its needs, said: "Let the children come to me . . . for to such belongs the kingdom of heaven."

THE CHILD MUST BE VIEWED IN HIS ENTIRETY

A child must be viewed in his entirety. One side of the child's growth cannot be studied in isolation, because a child grows as a whole being. He grows socially, physically, mentally, emotionally, and spiritually at the same time. Every phase of growth must be understood to guide and direct the total learning activities of the child and build in him attitudes for solid future living.

When one thinks of a kindergarten child, one must also think of what that child was during the years preceding his fifth birthday. In fact one must even go farther back and study carefully with what inherited qualities this child has been endowed. Heredity and the total environmental influences have left their impressions on the child and will continue to play an important part in the development and growth of his total being.

Consideration must also be given to the fact that today's young children live in a fast-moving, push-button age. Values are constantly changing. The children are better acquainted with the world and its problems than were their counterparts of several decades ago.

MANY FACTORS INFLUENCE GROWTH AND DEVELOPMENT

Even though the factors that influence the child's growth and development are many and varied, his home and family have wielded the greatest influence during these early years. The type of home in which the child grows up will, to a great extent, determine his attitude toward life and toward those who live with him. His relationship with his brothers and sisters, his place and status in the family — whether he is the firstborn, the middle or in-between child, or the baby — will all have some effect on his ability to get along with others and on his emotional responses toward life situations. The child's personal experiences with his father and mother, his grandparents, aunts, and uncles are extremely influential factors in determining character and outlook. Home relationships often set a pattern for the child's future behavior. Love and a feeling of security with wholesome affection will have beneficial effects on the child's whole character; while rejection, be it ever so slight, unkind criticism, and inconsistent discipline will be extremely harmful to the proper growth of the child.

To grow normally and fully, a child needs a secure status in the family group, that is, a feeling of belonging and a full acceptance of him by his family, just as he is, coupled with an understanding love and just and honest treatment.

THE TEACHER NEEDS TO UNDERSTAND THE CHILD'S PAST ENVIRONMENT

To understand a kindergarten child, a teacher will have to view the child in direct perspective with his past environment. She may wish to ask questions such as these:

1. Is the child a respected member of his family?
2. What is his place in the family?
3. Has he a normal relationship with his brothers and sisters?
4. Does he assume any responsibilities in the home?
5. Is he understood by his parents?
6. Is he receiving the love and attention that he needs?

7. Has he had normal experiences in keeping with his age?
8. Has he had a normal amount of success?
9. Is he perhaps smothered with love or parent domination?
10. Is he able to take a small amount of defeat?
11. Does he have a wholesome routine at home?

These and many other questions will help the interested teacher see her children in the light of their environment. They will help her set up a school environment in which the children can grow normally, not into "perfect ladies and gentlemen," but into wholesome boys and girls — alert, curious, and responsive.

A STUDY OF CHILDREN'S CHARACTERISTICS IS NECESSARY

After studying the background of the child, it will be necessary to study the character traits and attainments common to all normal children at or near the kindergarten stage of development.

It is true, no two children are alike, yet there are characteristics that all so-called normal children possess in a greater or lesser degree, and a wise teacher will want to watch if any child deviates too much from this accepted pattern. She must be careful, though, to judge the child according to his own particular growth pattern.

Five is a rather comfortable age. The child has come to the end of his rapid growth period, usually known as "early childhood." He has learned many skills, especially the large muscle skills, during this period and is now using them with some degree of efficiency. He has learned to walk, run, skip, hop, and jump and is able to climb a tree or a ladder and to walk up and down steps. He is beginning to play well with others. He has become familiar with his home environment, his neighbors, and his near neighborhood. He is manifesting a desire to be with other groups of children and adults. He shows a protective attitude toward smaller children and even enjoys sharing his toys with them for a short time. He still plays a lot with imaginary playmates and is still content to pass a great deal of his time playing alone.

The five-year-old is also developing his smaller muscles with some degree of success. He is becoming adept in handling crayons and paints and sometimes even a pencil.

He is attempting to tie knots and bows and fasten zippers, and he is able with some assistance to dress and undress himself, both with indoor and outdoor clothes.

He knows his own left and right hand fairly well but is not yet able to tell those of others, or follow directions to the left and to the right, or march in step. Most children at this age show signs of left- or right-hand dominance.

In communicating the kindergarten child is beginning to handle the language well. He is learning to express ideas and is able to carry on an intelligible conversation with adults and also with his peers. He already has had considerable practice with the spoken language before he comes to school. It has been estimated that some kindergarten children speak from 7,500 to 10,500 words and have, therefore, a set of growth patterns already pretty securely fixed. The opposite is also true. Some children possess meager vocabularies under which they struggle.

The kindergarten child is inquisitive and seeks information by asking many questions such as:

> What makes it snow?
> Where do chickens come from?
> Why do airplanes fly?
> Why do bees sting?
> Who made God?

His questions are gradually becoming fewer, but they are more relevant than they were a year or two earlier. He is beginning to ask for the sake of gaining information, and for this reason his questions are more meaningful.

A child of kindergarten age has a keen memory and delights in telling stories and personal experiences, remembering the smallest details. He can usually tell his first and last name and often his address and his father's name.

The normal five-year-old talks without articulation and has a limited exchange of ideas. In conversation he cannot suppress his point of view long enough to try to understand others.

He is able to count by rote to 19 or 20 without help, sometimes going on to 100 with help at the deciles. Many a child at this age has a good intelligent concept of numbers and uses it in everyday living.

A kindergarten child can draw a man with differentiation of parts, and draws other figures from his own experiences quite freely in outline form. The figures on the following page illustrate drawings of a normal five-year-old.

The aforementioned standards are but guideposts that have been set up through research in growth and development of small children. Though these expectancies of growth must be studied well and reflected on, they must not be used to make arbitrary boundaries for the growth of the kindergarten child. Despite these common characteristics, the command of the language and its use will vary greatly from child to child, and each child will continue to grow at his pace.

INDIVIDUAL DIFFERENCES MUST BE CONSIDERED

A teacher of children must ever remain aware that God, the almighty Creator, has made each child an individual personality with special powers, peculiar weaknesses, and particular needs, and that each child follows his own particular pattern of growth and will develop according to this pattern.

Although normal children are essentially similar in their sequence of growth, no two children, even in the same family, are alike in the way in which they pass through these sequences. Nor do they pass through the various stages at the same age or at the same time. Growth is a continuous process, and progress is not made abruptly as a child passes from month to month and from year to year. A teacher must remember that each child is functioning at some time at a particular maturity level, but that no two of her children reach the same level at the same time or in the same way.

If a teacher recognizes the fact that no two children are ever alike in their growth pattern, she will realize that she dare not expect the same development, the same behavior, or the same achievement from all the children in her group. A Christian kindergarten teacher will be conscious of the individuals whom God has created, and she will willingly accept the responsibility to provide an environment for all her children and plan a program of study that will meet the needs of every child in her class. She will give each

little boy and girl the right to develop normally and successfully according to the way in which he is to grow.

Children do pass through certain stages of growth. This is not determined by chronological age but by the child's individual pattern of growth. A concern for the correct evaluation of each child's present developmental and achievement level will give the teacher a basis for further guidance.

An understanding of the various "types" of children who may not follow a somewhat regular growth pattern will also assist in individual program planning. A "type" classification does not necessarily place a child into a category but merely makes it possible for a teacher to notice certain characteristics and personality traits as the child moves through these phases of development.

The *shy child,* who is apparently afraid to do anything, especially anything new, and who seems to withdraw from the association of other children, needs to gain confidence in himself. If he first gains confidence in the teacher, he will be more ready to build it in himself. The teacher will lead him slowly, through kindness, to feel important and needed in the group. She will try to find small tasks at which the child can succeed and then praise him publicly for his achievement. He needs a lot of praise and commendation and must never, not even for the poorest work or effort, be ridiculed, laughed at, or pushed aside to give place to a more aggressive or talented child.

The shy little child must be led to experience the full love of God and learn to trust Him implicitly. From trust in God and His protection, and from trust in his teacher, he can slowly be led to trust others and then also to have faith in himself.

The *aggressive* or *self-willed child,* who is usually recognized by his "bossy" ways, is a child who needs help rather than repression and domination. Self-will and rebellion in a child are often the reverse side of that good quality in a child, a desire for independence. What seems like bossiness in small children is perhaps the beginning sign of leadership, only that the child has not yet learned how and when to use leadership qualities. It is the teacher's God-given task to lead and guide this child into the proper channels, so as not to cripple his potential leadership qualities but, at the same time, to direct him in consideration toward others and in proper respect for divine and human authority.

The aggressive child must be taught to respect the rights and feelings of others and to realize that a real leader also knows how to follow. This realization can usually be developed by consistent Christian social living within the group. The aggressive child must have an opportunity to do many things, things that are of a challenging nature. If he finds worthwhile activities at which he can use his ingenuity and his aggressive ways, he will spend his time at these activities rather than in dominating other children for the want of something to do.

If worthwhile, the ideas of the aggressive child should be accepted and used, especially if he has shown a cooperative spirit and a willingness to work with the group. He wants to please and wants to be accepted but because of a lack of knowledge does not yet know just how to get his views across except by getting his way. If guided rightly, this child will soon respond favorably. It will take time, for many undesirable traits will have to be replaced by more desirable ones. Patience on the part of the teacher will speed up the change of behavior. Care must be taken, though, when trying to redirect self-will, not to crush strength of character.

The *immature child,* who has not grown up as fast as other children of the same age, may be physically immature, or he may be socially or emotionally immature. Regardless of the area of his immaturity, he will have problems peculiar to himself. The teacher will first of all have to recognize the fact that immaturity is not synonymous with lack of intelligence. An immature child may have just as keen a mind as a fully mature child, but he has not yet reached the stage of development at which the other children have arrived. The child may have been born prematurely and needs added years to reach normal development. His growth may have been retarded through illness, or he may be a slow-maturing child. Some children remain immature because their mothers prefer to keep them thus. The parents may cater to every wish and fancy, do everything for them, and prevent normal development. Some children, though they are few, do not want to grow up. They find more pleasure in staying babies and in acting accordingly.

No matter what the cause for immaturity may be, the child has a problem. On entering kindergarten he finds himself in a world of little folks who can do things much better and much faster than he can, and at once he becomes discouraged, runs to the teacher for help, or cries at the first sign of defeat. He often tries to reassure himself by asking the teacher, "Is this the way?" or "Is this right?" and even seeks help in picking out the toys with which he wants to play.

Harsh, severe treatment will not help the immature child grow up. If immaturity is from normal causes, it is wise to let time help the child develop. His growth dare not be forced by unkind treatment, for he cannot change his basic pattern and rate of growth. If the child is merely slow in losing his baby ways, he can be helped by encouraging him to try things alone and giving recognition where needed. Shaming or teasing treatment will not hasten independence. Telling the child that he is a baby will only hurt him. He will have to be accepted at the stage of development at which he has arrived and be helped from there on. All the experiences that he has missed will have to be offered to him. As he passes through each new stage of development, he will slowly but happily mature. It may take years before he reaches normality, but no amount of ridicule will force maturity. It may in fact retard it.

A teacher must be on guard never to compare unkindly the immature child's growth with that of others. She should help the child realize that people are to be loved and respected even if they are smaller or less able to do things. The kindest thing to do is help where help is needed, and let the child perform those tasks he can do well, slowly challenging him to do more and more by setting standards of achievement that are high, yet attainable for him.

The *overimaginative child,* formerly dubbed "lying child," possesses a super-amount of imagination. Because he is not able to differentiate between truth and make-believe, he often tells things that are not true but are merely fancies of his own imagination. He is not deliberately telling an untruth and will, if tactfully approached on the subject, readily admit that the story is just as he would "like it to be." At times the story seems real to him because he lives so much in the fairy-land and make-believe world that the line of demarcation between this land and his real life is not too clear.

When a child distorts facts and tells tall stories because they seem true to him, the problem is not so much one of sin as of helping him distinguish between fact and fiction. This takes time and patience. The full confidence of the child must be gained before he can be directed. He must know that you understand and that you are willing to listen to him. After his confidence has been gained, he may be reminded, before he starts to tell his story, "the way it really is"; or he may be asked, "Is this a real story, or is it make-believe?" If reminded gently each time he starts to relate his stories, he will soon drop his fanciful tales and direct his imagination into other channels, such as dramatic art, drawing, painting, and later into creative writing. The trait to be fanciful, therefore, need not be abolished, but rather directed, as it may be the beginning of a valuable creative ability.

The *egocentric* or *spoiled child* has often been a victim of an unfortunate home environment. Sometimes overindulgent parents and grandparents have showered so much attention on the child that he thinks it is only natural for everyone to bow to his wishes. He therefore makes all kinds of demands and tries to enforce them by whining, nagging, kicking, yelling, or displaying temper in one form or another.

Sometimes older brothers or sisters have taunted the child so much that he has learned to react with the methods mentioned above to gain sympathy or recognition from them. The egocentric child has a hard time adjusting to the boys and girls at school. He has become selfish and even delights in hurting other children. He does not care for the teacher's approval nor that of the group and appears contented even when separated from them. He has not learned acceptable ways of gaining recognition, and his unacceptable ways end in disappointment for him and result in his being disliked. When trying to help a child in this predicament, the teacher will first have to try to find out the reasons for his behavior, and then try to treat the cause. She might check back on his home environment and see if she can find the underlying cause there. She may have to speak quite frankly with the parents and solicit their wholehearted cooperation.

A spoiled child may respond to love and friendly attention on the part of the teacher, or it may be necessary to take stronger preventive measures with some unpleasant association. Separation from the group, denying him a privilege, taking away part of his playtime, speaking to him very firmly, or asking him to remain at home until he can work cooperatively with the other children, will at times bring results. The punishment, however, must not be merely of a punitive nature but must help the child become more and more trained in self-control and self-discipline. He must learn that complying with the wishes of the group and obeying those who are in charge can also be fun. Moreover, forms of punishment must vary according to the situation and must never be given in an angry, resentful mood. A teacher of small children dare never feel that a child is sinning against her personally, but must accept the act objectively and proceed from there.

Bible stories will have a beneficial influence on the egocentric child if he can be made to feel that he too can do as these men of God if he will but try and pray and ask God to help him do a little better every day.

The spoiled, selfish child must be made to feel that he is loved, even though he is troublesome and naughty. He must be made to feel that in times when he himself cannot control his actions you are right there to help. Do not make him feel that you have been disappointed in him or that he has failed, but rather compliment him on his little successes. Each time he controls his temper a bit more,

each time he is a little more friendly toward other children, he should be commended. Let him feel keenly that right actions are justly rewarded with a smile, a pat on the back, an extra privilege, and he will soon want to replace the undesirable ones with those more desirable. The child will forget many times, and therefore a great amount of patience will be necessary. It will pay. Expect a setback at times, and pay no great attention to it. Keep right on guiding and leading him with the love of God, kindness, and understanding. Never let this child feel that your love is contingent on his good behavior. Love him at all times.

The *indifferent child* or *lazy child* is found in most kindergarten groups. He seldom cares to participate in activities unless coerced to do so, and then he often takes part only halfheartedly. He tires easily, or at least appears to do so, and frequently assumes bodily positions of indifference—head on the table, head on his hands, arms stretched in the air, feet sprawled out—and he yawns many times during the day. Before passing the judgment of laziness on this child, a teacher will want to find out the reason for his attitude and observe the child in all situations—at work, at play, alone, with other children, and at home, if possible. The teacher will try to find out if the child is consistently indifferent or just spasmodically so.

The child may be disinterested in certain phases of work. He may not care for the physical activities, or he may dislike certain other school activities or procedures. A disinterested or indifferent child is quickly detected as a rule and can quite easily be changed in the course of time. Motivation on the part of the teacher, a little heart-to-heart talk with the child, a more friendly attitude on the part of the other children, or the finding of a playmate in the group may all have a wholesome effect on the child's disposition.

If the difficulty is deep-seated, it will be more difficult to detect and correct. The child may actually be fatigued from lack of sleep, lack of food, faulty elimination, centers of infection, poor eyesight, hearing disabilities, spinal injury, or sinus trouble and may not be able to respond in a normal manner.

A conference with the parents may bring underlying causes to light. The teacher should speak freely with them, make observations known, and suggest ways and means to correct some of the child's abnormalities. Parents are often so used to the behavior of their children that they do not see weaknesses until attention is drawn to them by someone else.

Physical weaknesses are somewhat easier to detect than deficiencies that arise from an unhappy emotional situation. The cause of the latter is sometimes hard to determine and still harder to correct. Many children come from broken or jarred homes, where the little one never felt secure. They have been cared for by nurses, sitters, relatives, friends, but never by a loving father or mother. Being taken care of by so many different people causes confusion for the child. Different people expect him to do different things. In trying to please them all, he never becomes habituated and feels totally insecure. His routine has never been established, and he is at a loss as to what to do and what not to do. As a result he does nothing. He plays the part of the lazy boy, knowing that thus he can get by without doing something wrong. He is playing it safe.

The indifferent child's attitude will have to be changed entirely and his whole outlook made more wholesome. If possible, the home situation should be changed, and often this can be achieved, at least in a measure, through proper counseling with the parents. If that is impossible, then at least the child should be given a happy, pleasant day at school, full of fun and laughter. A secure, free-from-care atmosphere at school will let him come out of his shell gradually, at his own rate of speed. He should experience many small successes and learn to take things as they come, grad-

ually learning to be a good sport, and learning to face life successfully and confidently. He will soon learn that when parents fail, his friends, his teachers, and his Savior will stand by. This type of child, too, can enjoy a happy childhood but must be handled with extreme care, conscientiousness, and wisdom.

The *superior child,* or the fast-learning child, often creates a problem in a group of average kindergarten children, and teachers wonder what they should do with this seemingly "disturbing" child. This child sometimes acts completely bored or delights in tormenting the other children.

Perhaps one side of this child's development has progressed faster than the others. He may have matured mentally or socially a year or two ahead of the group. If that is the case, the wise teacher will set her demands for achievement higher for this child than for the rest. She will let him feel that it is a privilege to do a little more work and that she expects better work from him because it is easier for him. Sometimes a child has matured mentally but is retarded physically, emotionally, or socially. Much time may then be spent in fostering activities that will help the child develop in these areas also. The kindergarten curriculum should be planned to stimulate and challenge the faster learner, yet not to defeat the slow achiever.

What if a child of this type has learned to read or is ready to read? There is no hard-and-fast rule as to when a child should learn to read, and if a child has learned from sisters and brothers or because he wanted to, give him an opportunity to read simple stories to the children. Give him some challenging pre-primers that he can read for fun, and allow him to find many hours of pleasure in just browsing through books. Let the child read or help you read stories and charts. This will take care of the desire to use newly learned skills and still will not set one child up as a pattern for the rest to try to follow. Place no reward on the achievement or make the children feel that it is necessary to read to be liked. Reading when fostered in a relaxed natural situation is a wholesome kindergarten activity.

Let the superior child also assist the children who are less able. This will help him occupy his time and train him in responsibility. But never let the child develop or display an arrogant attitude toward the other children. Show him that God has given all talents and that we must thank Him for them and never think less of less gifted children. Pride is directly contrary to the Christian spirit and needs to be discouraged, also in children.

The *slow-learning child* will also be found in the kindergarten. These children, too, can grow happily and successfully within their very own pattern. They need more time to learn than the average child. There is nothing different in appearance or in responses from the average child except for the fact that they learn more slowly and must therefore be taught more slowly. They will need careful, patient explanations, with a great amount of repetition and constant exercise of their skills.

These children, as all others, must be recognized as God's creatures and treated as such. They must never be subjected to ridicule of any kind and must receive recognition for tasks well done. Again the teacher will adjust the program to the individual needs of each particular child.

A slow-learning child usually remains slow-learning but will, with the teacher's help and guidance, be able to build a successful attitude toward his work provided he does not suffer too much defeat along the way. A child suffers defeat if standards for achievement are placed beyond his ability to reach.

The slow-learning child has perhaps already been subjected to nagging and criticism by parents or brothers and sisters. He will therefore doubly appreciate a teacher who understands him, who has faith in his ac-complishments, and who appreciates his small efforts and praises his limited contributions instead of constantly comparing him with his more fortunate playmates or brothers and sisters.

Since the child suffers keenly from harsh criticism and unkind comparisons, necessary criticism may be tempered by the use of softer terminology. For instance: When a child has done a piece of work completely wrong, one might say, "You might have done it this way," or "It would be better like this. Try it," rather than saying, "You did the whole thing wrong," or "Do it over; it's no good." This hurts and often stifles the child's initiative to do better or even to do anything at all. Success builds confidence, and the slow learner must have confidence in himself and in his own meager accomplishments to grow well.

The kindergarten child should be a happy child, and the kindergarten teacher should do everything in her power to help every child entrusted to her care live in a happy, cheerful environment, adjusted and tempered to his particular needs. She will consider it a privilege to be able to guide each child through his or her first school experience in an understanding way. A Christian teacher remembers that she is leading children to Christ and that these little ones entrusted to her, sinful though they be, have an inherent right to a happy, full, well-adjusted life here on earth. She will remember, above all, that they are heirs of heaven by right of their creation, redemption, and sanctification.

Each individual child will be a direct challenge to the teacher, who, aware of the problems and needs of all of them, will lead, guide, and direct them in the use of their creative powers and technical skills.

The kindergarten teacher will also use every opportunity to spread her philosophy of living and learning with children to others, realizing fully that the same Christian principles that are effective in the kindergarten are equally effective in teaching and guiding older children.

WHAT MIGHT BE EXPECTED FROM CHILDREN ENTERING KINDERGARTEN?

The child should—

Know his own name (given name and family name),

> his address,
> his telephone number, well enough to tell,
> if necessary.

Know how to take care of his toilet needs.

Be able to take care of his outer clothing, scarf, mittens, boots, and snow pants without assistance, except in difficult situations.

Know the way to and from school, and around his own neighborhood.

Be able to watch and obey traffic signals, policemen, and patrol boys.

Be able to go up and down steps with one foot on each step if possible.

Know how to use cleansing tissue properly, and to cover his mouth when coughing or sneezing.

Be willing to be away from home for several hours during the day without concern.

Be free from baby talk and able to carry on a conversation quite freely.

Keep fingers and objects out of his mouth.

Be free from displaying temper tantrums and undue fears.

Know how to follow simple directions.

Be able to put things away after using them.

Be interested in books and stories.

Children differ greatly in rate of growth in various abilities, and parents differ widely in the things they teach their children and in the independence they allow them to develop. It becomes necessary, therefore, for the teacher to view each child in the light of his own background. The above goals are merely suggested accomplishments that might be achieved in the prekindergarten years.

SIMPLE PRINCIPLES TO REMEMBER IN WORKING WITH SMALL CHILDREN

Give the children a feeling of security in every situation. Many things are new and frightening to them.

Offer sympathy only when it is really needed. Take a matter-of-fact attitude toward small bumps and bruises.

Give the children a *wholesome* amount of affection. Show a genuine liking for the child, but avoid sentimentality. Keep the teacher-pupil relationship from becoming too personal.

Be patient and calm. If you become excited, so will the child. Don't consider an offense as a personal act against you.

Have an unemotional attitude when difficulties arise. Be disturbed, if you must, but don't let the children know it. Better . . . don't get disturbed.

Help create and maintain an atmosphere that is free from strain. Find out what each child is able to do without pressure.

Avoid haste. Give the children plenty of time—use your judgment.

Do not stop abruptly the play or activities of a group. Keep a flexible, definite program. Strange, frequent changes may be disturbing.

Be consistent in handling situations. Children need to know what to expect under various circumstances.

Let the Word of God and the teachings of the Master Teacher, Jesus, be your constant guide.

Be honest and fair. Children are quick to judge insincerity or partiality.

Respect the children's rights and privileges. Treat them with courtesy.

Study the individual child and, when needed, use disciplinary measures that will be most effective with each particular child.

Provide necessary release for unacceptable behavior.

Correction should be immediate and firm, but just and of short duration. Be sure the child understands his misdemeanor. Do, don't just threaten. "We can't use you for awhile. Come, sit over here." When you isolate, do it in the room. Never send the child out. Separate him from the group for only a short time.

Love and respect your children as children of God.

**MY PERSONAL CHECKLIST OF ITEMS
TO REMEMBER ABOUT THE KINDERGARTEN CHILD**

3. The Kindergarten Environment

Happy hearts and happy faces,
Happy play in grassy places,
That was how, in ancient ages,
Children grew to Kings and Sages.
— *Robert Louis Stevenson*

KINDERGARTEN MEANS AN IMPORTANT CHANGE IN ENVIRONMENT

For five years little boys and girls have lived in their homes free to run and play at any time; free to roll and tumble on the floor; and free to rest when tired, eat when hungry, and cry when hurt.

Quite suddenly these children are taken from this accustomed environment and placed into a school situation, a place where one must do what others do, eat when told to, and often even go to the bathroom at the teacher's orders. This is a big change for the average five-year-old child, especially for the child who has had no preschool experience.

THE KINDERGARTEN SHOULD RESEMBLE A HOME

To make the change from home to kindergarten easy for the little boys and girls, a kindergarten room should resemble a home, a place where children will actually feel at home. The room should be like a big living room, not a parlor, to be looked at or admired, but a real room in which to live. It should be a friendly place that will offer opportunities for the child to plan, to think, to discover, to share, to play, and to explore—a place that will be conducive to Christian living and learning in real-life situations. It should be a workshop—a discovery center.

Very few kindergarten rooms can be classed as ideal when judged from the standpoint of space allotment for each child, correct lighting, exposure to direct sunlight, floor covering, windows, and other physical features. But every kindergarten room should still be made as nearly ideal as possible. Much will depend on the space allotted and the conditions existing in each particular case. The location and size of the room, condition of the walls, type of windows, lighting, equipment, play area, funds available, and many other local problems will have to be faced and solved when planning.

Some kindergarten rooms are multiple-use rooms, which must be reconverted from choir room or general meeting room day after day. The teacher who has to "set up" the room each morning and "pack it away" at night has added difficulties, but these too can be overcome until more adequate facilities can be provided.

So many factors influence the type of room that no attempt is made here to set up a standard. Very often the kindergarten room will be determined by the existing physical plant and by the available equipment. But let it be remembered that most rooms can be made attractive and functional.

The suggestions that follow are designed, therefore, to aid the teacher and others responsible for setting up the environment. The kindergarten room should be as attractive and workable as the environment will permit. Emphasis should be placed on the important features that make for wholesome living.

FEATURES OF A GOOD KINDERGARTEN ROOM

A good kindergarten room should have a purpose, a reasonable amount of order, and great flexibility. The room needs to be large enough to allow children to move around easily and to live and learn together without regimentation.

To make the exit and entrance easily accessible, both to the parents and the children, the room should be near the main entrance. If possible it should not be too close to an upper-grade classroom, for normal noise and activity in a kindergarten may be annoying to older children.

A room slightly longer than it is wide lends itself well to informal activities and is easier to make livable.

A kindergarten room should allow plenty of light for the children, whose eyes are not yet fully developed and who need a cheerful atmosphere in which to grow.

The walls in a kindergarten room are best finished with a nonglaze paint that can easily be cleaned and is easy on the eye. The color of paint will be determined to a great extent by the room exposure and by the teacher's preference, creativity, and ingenuity.

Ordinarily, soft greens or delicate pastels are used in rooms that receive much sunshine, especially southern or eastern exposures. Yellow in its various tints may be used to compensate for a lack of natural sunshine and light in northern or western exposures.

Some teachers prefer to have a dominant color with a secondary color and brightened with an accent, but this same effect of contrast can be achieved by proper decorations, such as draperies, rugs, chair coverings, and pictures.

Some concern should be shown for provision of satisfactory acoustics in the kindergarten room.

THE KINDERGARTEN FLOOR

Proper floor covering can provide for some sound absorption. However, the ideal kindergarten floor has not yet been determined. The material used, be it tile or carpeting, should be suited to hard wear and easy to clean. A concern should be that the floor is warm and draft-free, for much of the children's time will be spent on the floor. A wooden or cement floor can be covered with a large rug on which the children may play and gather for stories and play and singing. This not only provides the necessary warmth but gives a homelike atmosphere to the room. A heavily waxed floor is to be avoided. Though it might be the pride and joy of the custodian, it would only detract from the comfort and safety of the children.

WINDOWS

The outdoors is always fascinating to little children. They are happy to watch the other children at play, even when they themselves are not able to be outdoors. They delight in watching the birds, flowers, animals, and weather conditions through the windows. Therefore, whenever possible the windows in the kindergarten room should be low enough to allow the children to look out while they relax and leisurely go about their work and play. It is desirable to have windows on two sides, but not necessary. If they present a hazard, low windows should be protected with guard rails.

PLUMBING

A lavatory built in the kindergarten room is advantageous, though not necessary. It should, however, be close by. The children should have a period of their own in which to use it, without the disturbance of older children sharing it with them.

A drinking fountain in or near the room is desirable, because it would eliminate the "line up and drink" procedure and would encourage the children to drink when thirsty rather than when they are led to the fountain. A utility sink has a distinct advantage, for it can be used in case of accidents and also for any activities that require water.

BULLETIN BOARDS AND CHALKBOARDS

The kindergarten should have ample display space. Children love to live in an environment that they have created with their own drawings and pictures of their choosing. The bulletin boards should not be more than 20 or 22 inches from the floor, so that every child may help decorate and easily view the displays. A chalkboard should be accessible so the children can experiment with chalk at their leisure.

ARTIFICIAL LIGHTING

Almost all rooms need some type of artificial lighting. Care should be taken so that there is good distribution of the light. The exact amount of artificial light needed can be determined, and lighting experts should be consulted.

EQUIPMENT

Sometimes the facilities that are to be used for a kindergarten room are beyond one's control and must be accepted. But regardless of the room facilities, the equipment should be good and usable.

LOCKERS

Each child should have an individual locker space—if possible, a place that will hold his coat and some of his treasured supplies. If plain hooks are used for the coats and hats, then some spacious, neat, open cupboards should be provided for such materials as crayons, rugs for resting, smocks, cleansing tissues, and the like. Names should be printed in manuscript letters on or above the lockers. Suitable lockers are illustrated.

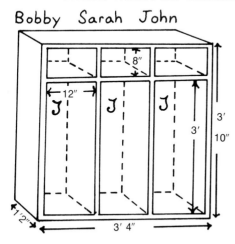

Lockers

CHAIRS AND TABLES

Kindergarten children should not be expected to sit at fixed desks but should have movable furniture, tables, and chairs of different heights. Chair heights are usually 12 inches, 13 inches, and 14 inches, with an average of 13 inches, depending on the size of the children.

The tables should be wide enough to allow children to work opposite one another, for they are vitally interested in what others are doing. By sitting opposite one another, the children can also learn to share in the use of materials and at the same time learn from one another. The correct distance between the seat of the chair and the tabletop is about 9½ inches. Tabletops should be washable and durable.

It is advisable to have a few extra chairs and tables for centers of interest—a library corner, a science table, or a painting area. It will not be necessary to have tables for all the children to use at the same time, especially if the room is small. The children can work in groups, one group using the tables, while others use the floor or the boards and easels.

The teacher's desk, rarely used when the children are in the room, need not be large and need not occupy a prominent place in the room. If the room is small, it may be pushed into a corner of the room. Furniture should be arranged with imagination.

SHELVES

Wide shelves should be built low enough for the children to keep their toys: trucks, fire engines, toy carts, airplanes, tractors, farm animals, dolls, and games of all kinds. The children can then be made to feel responsible for caring for these shelves themselves, for they can reach them and put things away in an orderly manner. Movable shelves, built in sections, make good dividers for work centers.

OTHER STORAGE SPACE

The teacher, too, ought to have ample storage space for her own supplies. Cupboards with doors are preferable. The shelves

or cupboards that hold everyday equipment, such as paste, paper, scissors, crayons, paints, or clay, should be open and low enough for the children to get the supplies easily and replace them carefully.

Everything that is not in daily use should be stored or discarded. The furniture in the room should be so arranged that one senses a feeling of balance and ease. The various centers of interest and activities may be distributed around the room, leaving plenty of free space for rhythms, games, and general moving about.

Blocks may be stored according to size in large wooden boxes with large casters, or trucks on wheels, or kept in a homemade drag box that the children can easily pull from place to place.

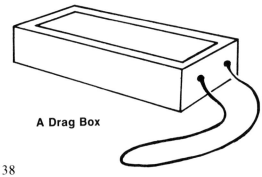

A Drag Box

MISCELLANEOUS EQUIPMENT

A dollhouse with furniture is always a welcome piece of furniture and a joy for many children. A workbench with some tools and a supply of wood is also an asset if the room is large and the group of children small. Little boys and girls need much care and guidance when working with tools, so this activity, though worthwhile, is not absolutely necessary. There are many activities that supply the same type of enjoyment and can be used as a substitute for the desire to saw and pound and make something. The alert teacher will constantly be searching for equipment that is challenging to the pupils and designed with sound educational principles in mind.

A piano is helpful but not absolutely necessary provided the teacher can carry a tune. A record player with selected records is almost indispensable. A tape recorder and an overhead projector add to the efficiency of teaching.

An easel or two should be placed close to the sink, and a rack for paper ought to be near the easel so that the children may feel free to draw and paint without too much effort in getting things ready. The floor lends itself well to this activity.

FURNITURE IN A MULTIPLE-USE ROOM

In case the room is a multiple-use room, the furniture and equipment will have to be chosen with great care, for they will have to be stored in a minimum of space when not in use.

Lightweight screens, 4 feet by 6 feet, can serve as bulletin boards and still be used to divide centers of interest during the day and cover the stored furniture by night. Chairs in this case should be of the folding type. They will not take up much room when stored. Shelves and tables may be on rollers. If moving is made easy, some of the larger children in the school can be taught to arrange the room for the teacher. Even the early comers will enjoy helping the teacher get the room ready. A room such as this should serve only as a temporary arrangement, and plans should be made to provide better facilities as soon as possible.

TEMPERATURE AND HUMIDITY

Wherever and whatever the room may be, care should be taken that it is a healthy place in which to live. It must not be damp or cold. The best temperature is from 67 to 70 degrees Fahrenheit. The thermometer or thermostat belongs at the breathing level of the children when seated to be certain that the room is warm where the children play and work. The relative humidity should be kept between 30 and 40 in a room of normal temperature. Pans of water may be placed on the radiator if the room is too dry, until a more modern ventilating system can be acquired.

ORDER IN THE ROOM

The small child loves routine and grows well when kept in routine; therefore, the general arrangement of the room ought not to be changed too frequently. Since children expect to find things where they left them the day before, it is not a wise idea to change the furniture while the children are away. If a change has to be made, it should be made together with the children. They might also suggest and help with the arrangement.

The room in general is to be neat and clean, pleasing to look at, but not over-stimulating.

There should be a place for everything. It is extremely important that the children learn to know the proper places, so that they can put things away where they belong. It is not always an easy matter to keep a kindergarten room looking neat and tidy and at the same time carry on stimulating activity. While the room is a workshop, a certain amount of neatness must be maintained at all times, or the children will become distracted or confused. It should, however, reflect the fact that children are living in it.

The children can be taught to feel a certain degree of responsibility in keeping the room neat. They can do little tasks according to their ability. The teacher will then make the final checkup to see that things are in order for the next day.

In the morning, too, she will again put on the finishing touches to make the room a ready place for little, eager people to live. She may arrange the shades, look after the plants, set out a few interesting things for the children, and, in general, check over everything.

PETS

Growing and living things in a room add much to the enjoyment of the children and arouse an interest in God's creatures. They also give the children an opportunity to care for them, thus accepting their share of responsibility. Turtles, fish, a canary, gerbils, or a rabbit at Eastertime all might be welcome visitors in a kindergarten room. If adequate facilities and care can be provided, permanent pets may also be a possibility.

MISCELLANEOUS EQUIPMENT

Toy telephones, dust mops and brooms, a small cooking stove, a washing machine, a clothesline with clothespins, and a cupboard with dishes all have a place in the kindergarten room. Trucks, fire engines, hot rods, jets, rockets, and balls should have a prominent place.

WORSHIP CENTER

If the teacher desires a corner in the room for worship, she may have a small table serve as an altar or have a small altar made out of a box and covered with an appropriate cloth. A cross may be placed on it, perhaps next to a large Bible with pictures in it. Candles or flowers may be placed on the altar and a religious picture hung behind the altar. The worship center should be kept plain and in harmony with the small child's thinking. It should be changed from time to time.

SOCIAL CLIMATE IS IMPORTANT

Far more important than any equipment or room arrangement is the social climate that exists in the room. Social climate is hard to describe, yet it can be sensed almost immediately upon stepping into the room. It is revealed by the relationship that exists between the teacher and the pupils and among the pupils themselves.

In an ideal situation the children seem free and easy, yet never uncontrolled. They feel secure under the guiding hand of an understanding teacher who knows when to step into the picture to settle a quarrel, referee an argument, suggest improvement, teach a worthwhile truth, dry some tears, take a disturbing member out of the group, or forbid something contrary to the Christian way of life. She also seems to know when and how to give the children small doses of her own greater fund of knowledge and lead them into new experiences without stifling their own initiative.

This social climate is nothing tangible, nothing one can write down and memorize, but is created largely by the spirit and personality of the teacher herself and caught and reflected by the children. She will set the atmosphere for wholesome, Christian living and learning.

THE TEACHER IS IMPORTANT

Next to the children the kindergarten teacher is the most important part of the program. She must guide the children into the Christian life. She sets the climate of the room and sets the stage for learning. It is her task to inspire the boys and girls to want to learn and to help them experience the joy of discovery. She sets the standards and goals and is an important influence in building attitudes and character traits in the children. She is the major factor in helping the children make successful adjustments to school life.

Since she makes the initial contact with the parents, she must build a foundation for good public relations. She may have the privilege of introducing the parents to the church family.

She is also responsible for constructing a program based on sound learning principles and a Christian philosophy of education. She must adjust the program to the needs of each child and then execute it so that each child will move ahead both in cognitive learnings and in the development of a Christian personality.

Many beginning teachers, struggling with problems of behavior and classroom control, look with wonder at some experienced teacher who apparently seems able to control her group with little or no effort. They wonder by what miracle this teacher achieves such a smooth-running classroom.

The experienced teacher knows full well that her success is not miraculous. It is the result of careful planning, of a keen understanding of childhood gained from years of observing and studying, and of an unswerving devotion to the cause for which she works.

An interested, intelligent, consecrated teacher can be successful in establishing a social climate that will reflect true Christian living, if she keeps her ideals before her and uses all possible means to reach them. She must gain a proper perspective toward her work and build a proper sense of values within herself. Some things she must place first and foremost and strive to reach these goals.

QUALITIES OF A GOOD TEACHER

A teacher in a Christian kindergarten who wishes to guide children to growth in Christian living must herself be a sincere Christian with deep spiritual resources from which she can draw strength and comfort. She must use all these resources frequently, and she must realize that she is planting the seed and that God through His Holy Spirit will give the increase. Thus, she will know that God is ever at her side to bless her and her efforts.

If she is truly filled with the love of Christ, she will sincerely try to exemplify this love through her actions toward her children, toward those with whom she works, and toward the parents and friends of the school.

Next to being a real Christian, she should be a real person—a happy, understanding, patient person. She needs to be young in spirit and young enough in years to be able to enter wholeheartedly into the children's activities, yet mature in judgment, so that the parents will have full confidence in her as a person and in her philosophy, her ideals, and her procedures.

One of the most important traits in a teacher of young children is her sensitivity to each child's needs. It is extremely important that the teacher is familiar with the developmental characteristics of children at various growth levels. She should be a broadly educated person in knowledge and appreciation.

This does not mean, however, that she must smother the children with affection and overconcern. She must be genuinely fond of them, with a deep concern for their proper growth and development. She must be kind and loving, yet definite and just in her actions toward them. She sets standards that they can successfully reach and expects them to meet the challenge without coaxing or begging. Children usually respond to quiet expectancy on the part of the teacher more readily than they do to a lot of talking, pleading, or scolding.

The idea that a sugary, gracious manner with "Honey, this" and "Darling, that" is an indispensable asset has often caused teachers to concentrate so much on their own mannerisms that they have entirely lost sight of the children's needs. It is not necessary to refer to kindergarten children as "my happy little people" or "my dear kiddies" or to be reminding them constantly to act like "fairies" or "butterflies" or "birds." Young children want to be treated as human beings with sense and powers of reason, not like babies or toys. Treat them as healthy, growing children.

CHILDREN QUICKLY
APPRAISE THE TEACHER

Children are quick to catch the spirit and moods of a teacher. Her enthusiasm for her work will bring liveliness into the room; her sense of humor will bring relaxation; her attitude of friendly respect and affection will bring happiness; and her attitude of quiet, yet consistent, expectancy will bring attention and action.

With the right attitude toward the children, the teacher will make the boys and girls feel that they are loved at all times, regardless of their behavior. They will feel that she is ready and willing to help them when they are in trouble or when they lack in self-control or in powers of achievement.

Children are quick to sense any injustice or insincerity by the teacher and will react toward others much as the teacher acts toward

them. If the teacher is kind and sympathetic toward the slow learner or toward the otherwise handicapped child, the children are bound to react the same way. In this way a spirit of Christian love can be caught as well as taught.

CONTROL MUST BE MAINTAINED

A teacher will aim at all times to have control of her group and never let them feel her helplessness. She will calmly and unobtrusively change activities, read a story, or play a game until she has regained control.

Letting the children feel that she has lost control, or telling them so, would only rob her of the respect that she deserves and that she needs to lead and guide a group in effective living. She need never manifest a spirit of dominance, but should have a definiteness, which the children will catch and appreciate. Children thrive well when they accept and abide by routine—not a rigid, militaristic routine, but a free, orderly, relaxed way of doing things. She will feel free to discard regimented routines. Rather she will set up a relaxed, orderly code of living in which she respects children's ideas, stimulates curiosity, releases tensions, and allows opportunity for development.

A teacher will, through study and experience, learn to create a fitting balance between freedom and restraint, between play and responsibility. She will learn better to be a thought-provoking guide, a fair critic, and a wise counselor. She will grow in spiritual grace, with love toward God and man. She will increase her confidence in her own ways of doing things, her methods and procedures, and try to gain a better mastery of the essential techniques in guiding and teaching children. She will not lose sight of the fact that all education is a developmental process and that there is no man-made ideal by which all children are measured.

SOME THINGS TO REMEMBER

A KINDERGARTEN TEACHER will—

Read the Bible diligently, knowing that it is the source of Christian faith, strength, and wisdom.

Keep promises made to her children—or explain why they couldn't be kept.

Acknowledge her own mistakes.

Show friendliness with a quick smile or a pat on the back.

Know when to ignore and discount childish faults.

Know how much criticism or praise to give each child.

Remember that a slight indication of disapproval is more effective with some children than a severe rebuke is with others.

Administer punishments herself. (Only in the gravest emergencies will she call in a superior.)

Relate the punishment directly to the wrongdoing, to emphasize the relationship between cause and effect.

Punish immediately upon the wrongdoing. Children forget their misdeeds after a short time, and wonder why they are being punished.

Make the punishment of very short duration and constructive in manner. (Never punish when angry or out of revenge.)

Not depend on candy, stars, prizes, and what-have-you to maintain discipline or gain the love of the child.

Have the children realize that true rewards come from their satisfaction of having learned and worked well.

Not manifest an overmaternal attitude by frequently doing things for the children that they could well do for themselves.

Realize that her voice has a direct effect on the behavior of the children, and try to keep it pleasant, low, but alive, avoiding loud, strident, shrill tones, as well as weak, timid ones.

Watch that her movements about the room are not uncertain, which gives an appearance of helplessness. She will rather walk and move about confidently, appearing sure of herself.

Be concerned about her appearance, remembering that children like variety and color. This will not call for an elaborate wardrobe, but merely for an eye tuned to something pretty—a scarf, a tie, a flower, some beads, or a pin. All these attract the attention of children, for they like things that are pretty.

Do all in her power to stay physically fit, mentally alert, and emotionally stable. She will seize every opportunity to enjoy herself in wholesome recreation and physical activities, as well as to hear and see things that are pleasant and inspirational.

Not expect self-government in the kindergarten, for this requires a maturity that the five-year-olds do not have. Their memories are short, their control limited, and their judgment faulty. They are too young to understand all the facts involved in any one case.

Be on guard not to develop a stoical, negative attitude toward her children and their childish ways of reacting. She may become overcritical regarding nonessentials and fail to get the joy and satisfaction out of living and learning with young children.

Like parents and enjoy sharing her problems with them. She will welcome them as visitors and also visit with them in their homes.

Pray for her children and represent them before the Throne of grace. She will assure them of the love of God, who sent them a Savior from sin. Through example and teaching she will lead them ever closer to Him, so that their lives will be the happier and their adjustment to life the easier and more secure.

Accept a child at his particular phase of development and start at the point at which he has arrived. From there on, help him grow, regardless of where other children may be.

Never shame a child for slow growth or lack of maturation.

Never unduly force children to excel so as to glorify herself or her methods, but let them grow at an even, natural pace, free from tensions and fear. Challenge without pushing.

PART TWO

THE KINDERGARTEN
CURRICULUM

4. Christian Living and Learning

"Perhaps the most challenging task of any generation is the religious nurture of its children."

— *Rosemary Roorbach*

MANY KINDERGARTEN CHILDREN KNOW LITTLE ABOUT GOD

As a rule a little child who enters the kindergarten for the first time knows very little about God and His wonderful plan of salvation for mankind. Unless he has grown up in a Christian home or attended Sunday school, he has perhaps not even learned to talk with God in prayer.

From now on these little people with various religious backgrounds will be influenced directly by the environment in the Christian kindergarten. They will absorb impressions and build attitudes toward God and man from their day-to-day experiences. The Christian teacher by her life will help build a Christian philosophy in her children. They, in turn, will be ready to reflect her life in theirs.

THE TEACHER'S RESPONSIBILITY

In the light of this, one can readily see that a truly Christian atmosphere must be maintained throughout the day. Communion with God and applied Christian living must be guided, directed, and taught just as carefully as any other phase of growth. A child will not "just grow" spiritually by himself — he must be taught; not in a period a day, but all through the day. Worship, reverence, and many other Christian virtues cannot be regarded as "things to be done" during a specified time of the day. A consecrated teacher will use every opportunity to continuously build these attitudes in her children. She will utilize situations and, if necessary, create situations in which prayer life and God-pleasing ways of living together can be practiced.

To do this a teacher will maintain a wholesome attitude toward life, keep herself in good health, maintain abundant energy, pray for patience and love, develop a sense of humor and a sympathetic understanding for the little ones about her. She will often teach more by how she feels than by what she says. The feeling of joy, wonder, and awe over the marvelous truths of God's Word will be caught as well as taught. Every truth taught and learned will surely find application through the day in the many activities with the children.

THE BEGINNING OF RELIGIOUS INSTRUCTION

A little child is eager to learn. He wants to find out and will look forward with joy to a few moments every day which are set aside for "Time with God." A word of caution: These periods should be short and happy ones so that no child will feel that time with God is tiring, but will long for more moments spent in this way. The time may be increased as the children develop longer attention spans, but at the start the periods should be short. They should always be kept reverent, but relaxed.

It may be advisable, before leading the children into more or less formal religion lessons, to build up attitudes toward God through everyday experiences that lend themselves naturally to an interpretation of God and His wonderful world. Mother and father protection are examples of God's love and protection, and a child who has experienced the former can easily make a transfer from his parents' affection to the love of God. In the same way a sense of wonder, of being alive in God's great world, and a study of the lovely things in nature can stimulate in the child a love and respect for God. The natural laws — rain, thunder, snow, ice — and the wonders of space exploration with which the children have already had some experiences can help them develop a greater and clearer concept of God and His preservation.

Little acts of kindness at home and at school will help the children see more clearly the greater love of God to all men, for they will learn how love prompts us to do things for others. They can then more fully appreciate the great love of God, who sent His Son Jesus Christ into the world to save them and all men from their sins.

Learning to know Jesus in this way will help the children feel close to Him. They will become acquainted with a real Friend, a real Jesus. One should not miss these natural situations in life to lead the little ones to Him.

These life situations, together with appropriate stories, songs, prayers, and creative activities, will help develop a desire to learn more about God. Through the Holy Spirit they may come to a fuller acceptance of Jesus as their Savior.

OBJECTIVES OF KINDERGARTEN RELIGION

1. To gradually lead the child to a conscious faith in Jesus, his Savior.

2. To nurture the child's faith.

3. To lead the child to a conscious appreciation of God as His Creator and heavenly Father.

4. To help the child find joy in living and to associate all his happy experiences with God.

5. To help the child feel secure under God's loving care.

6. To help the child learn to trust in God and in His almighty power.

7. To help the child show his love and thankfulness to God by his response in worship, prayer, and living.

8. To help the child learn to love the church as God's family and the Bible as God's message.

9. To lead the child to realize his sin and his need for a Savior and to ask forgiveness from Jesus.

10. To lead the child slowly to appreciate chosen gems of God's Word — easy Bible verses and some simple hymn verses and prayers.

11. To develop in the child a desire and love to speak to Jesus in spontaneous prayer.

12. To help the child live under God's covenant — growing daily in grace and learning to respond with a love for his family and others.

A CURRICULUM FOR TODAY'S BOYS AND GIRLS

In this fast-moving world it gives us real security to know that, despite the rapid changes, God and His promises remain constant and absolute!

God expects us to carry on His mission in this rapidly changing world. To meet this challenge we must seek more efficient ways of communicating His love to our preschool children. We must be aware of new procedures, programs, Bible-centered materials, machines, and all multimedia that help us better to pursue our God-given goals.

Especially in the education of the young has there been a distinct shift from a passive receiving of teacher-given content to active participation. In religious education this type of teaching should find a wholesome response, since children are naturally active and want to participate.

Kindergarten teachers will want to check the new curriculum in religion entitled *Mission:Life* produced by the Board of Parish Education, The Lutheran Church — Missouri Synod, and available through Concordia Publishing House, St. Louis, Missouri 63118, in fall, 1971. This new program supplemented by materials found in the curriculum guides listed in the bibliography and built around the outline appearing later in this chapter should serve well as a basis for a kindergarten curriculum.

The teacher who is just beginning or who

wishes a sequential approach will find the outline a good guide or skeleton on which to build her program. She may add or delete in accordance with the maturity level of her particular group.

The outline calls for a great deal of repetition. Repetition is not boring to children. They love to repeat the things they know. They will love the things that become a part of them through repetition and will also remember them. The teacher should feel free to substitute songs, prayers, and Bible texts at any time for those suggested here. Songs may be sung at any time during the day — during a storm, for example, or on special occasions — and the children should be encouraged to speak to Jesus at any time.

MEMORY SELECTIONS

The unit outlines contain material from which selections may be chosen for memorizing. Memory selections, which may be Bible words, hymn stanzas, or prayers, should be used with discretion and according to the ability of the pupils. No memory work ought to be forced on young pupils, and every effort on their part, be it ever so small, ought to be accepted. Make no assignments for home study, and only work for very short periods at a time. Repeat day after day. Exactness in memorizing is not as important as the reaction of the child who hears the great truths. Exactness and "perfection" will follow as the child grows and increases in knowledge and comprehension. Build up a love for God's Word and a reverent attitude toward it.

PROCEDURE IN TEACHING

Do not adhere too strictly to any given form of procedure. Vary your methods of presentation lest your teaching become stereotyped and lose its personal touch.

1. One day you may tell the story.

2. Another time the children may tell small parts.

3. Children may ask questions on the story.

4. Flannelgraph presentations may be used.

5. One child may relate the whole story.

6. Filmstrips and overhead projectors are excellent teaching aids.

7. Records and cassettes of favorite Bible stories are a joy in a kindergarten classroom.

8. Dramatization that involves all the children is an excellent means of expression.

HANDWORK AND ACTIVITIES

After the great truths have been presented, it is good procedure to engage in handwork or in other activities related to the lesson. Children delight in acting out the story, drawing pictures, or cutting out and making things. Some activities have been listed for "starters." A creative teacher will find many more, and children, too, will promote their own original ideas. Any suggested patterns are only to serve as ideas from which to launch into activity with creativity.

When using activities in conjunction with your religion lessons, try to keep a unity of thought. Ask yourself the following:

1. Does the activity contribute definitely to the accomplishment of the desired goals?

2. Does it clarify a religious truth? Is it teaching — or just passing time?

3. Does it provide opportunities to practice Christian living?

4. Is it an expression of the children's own creativity?

It is not necessary for each child to work on the same activity at the same time. Let the children work in groups or individually, for in this way they will feel free to think, experiment, and create.

GET CHILDREN ACQUAINTED WITH THE BIBLE

Use the Bible as your main source in

religious instruction. Love it, read it, and tell it.

Let this be your guide:

1. Base every religious truth that you teach on the Bible.

2. Always treat the Bible as a very special Book. Let the children look at it and feel it. If it has pictures in it, show them to the children.

3. Read your memory verses from the Bible. Sometimes while telling your story, read a part from the Bible—just a verse or two. Perhaps a child may like to hold the Bible while you read from it.

4. Before you tell your story, open the Bible and talk about the story. Let the children realize that you have a book from God. Do not read the story to them. Tell it. Hold the Bible and refer to it as you tell the story.

5. Sometimes when you sing, refer to the Bible and show how songs also tell the love of Christ.

SUGGESTED OUTLINE

Since children at kindergarten age are still closely identified with their own families, it is a satisfying experience for them if this bond is extended into the first few weeks of school life. It is always wise to start with the familiar and move slowly toward new horizons. A unit on The Home and Family can well serve as the core for Religion and Social Studies (see Chapter 5 for ideas).

INTRODUCTORY UNIT
Families Are the Children of God
   A. I Belong to My Family—I Belong to God's Family
   B. My Friends Have Families—I Want My Friends to Be in God's Family
   C. There Are Many Different Families—There Are Many Bible Families

UNIT I
Jesus, the Children's Friend
   A. Little Children Visit Jesus
   B. Jesus Calls Children His Little Lambs
   C. Jesus Helps Sick Children
   D. Jesus Loves All Children Everywhere

UNIT II
God Cares for His Children
   A. God Makes All Things
   B. God Watches Over His Children
   C. God Sends His Angels to Watch His Children
   D. God Gives Us Our Food

UNIT III
Jesus Helps Many People
   A. Jesus Helps People When They Need Him
   B. Jesus Makes a Big Storm Stop
   C. Jesus Answers Prayer
   D. Jesus Helps the Blind to See

UNIT IV
God Sends His Son
   A. God Promises a Savior from Sin
   B. God Keeps His Promises
   C. God Sends the Christmas Baby
   D. Little Jesus Gets Christmas Gifts

UNIT V
Jesus Grows Up
   A. Mary and Joseph Trust in God's Protection
   B. Jesus Goes to Church
   C. Jesus Teaches About God's Love
   D. Jesus Heals the Sick

UNIT VI
Jesus Takes Our Sins Away
   A. People Hurt Jesus
   B. Jesus Lives Again
   C. Jesus Shows Himself to His Friends
   D. Jesus Goes Home to Heaven

UNIT VII
Jesus Teaches Us
   A. God's Children Help Others
   B. Jesus Forgives Sins
   C. God's Children Gladly Hear His Word
   D. Jesus Teaches Us to Pray

UNIT VIII
God's Children Love Jesus
   A. God's Children Praise Jesus
   B. God's Children Serve Him
   C. God's Children Show Love to Others
   D. God's Children Do God's Will

UNIT IX
People Who Loved God
   A. Men of Faith
   B. Men of Trust
   C. Mighty Preachers
   D. Great Missionaries

UNIT OUTLINES

The sources of songs, prayers, and activities have been abbreviated in the outlines as follows:

LH — *The Lutheran Hymnal*

CGS — *A Child's Garden of Song*

LCSG — *Little Children, Sing to God!*

CGP — *A Child's Garden of Prayer*

LFH — *Little Folded Hands*

CK — *The Christian Kindergarten (Note. The CK references are to the older*

edition of *The Christian Kindergarten)*

FF — *Finger Fun* (Cincinnati: Standard Publishing Co.)

FFF — *Fascinating Finger Fun* (Grand Rapids, Mich.: Zondervan Publishing House)

TBF — *Ten Busy Fingers* (Philadelphia: Fortress Press)

The numbers after each abbreviation indicate page numbers.

In addition to the suggestions provided here, consult *Mission:Life* curriculum materials, *Joyfully Sing*, and other useful publications.

UNIT I
JESUS, THE CHILDREN'S FRIEND

Aim:

That the children may learn to know and love Jesus as their personal Friend.

A. Little Children Visit Jesus
Bible Stories:

Jesus Blesses the Children. Mark 10: 13-16; Luke 18:15-17

Jesus and a Little Child. Matt. 18:1-14

Anticipated Learnings:

Jesus loves all children.

Jesus loves me.

Songs:

Jesus Loves Children. *CGS* 76

Jesus Loves Me, This I Know. *LCSG* 16

Jesus, Friend of Little Children. *LCSG* 19

My Best Friend Is Jesus. *LCSG* 20

Jesus Loves the Little Children. *LCSG* 75

I Am Jesus' Little Lamb. *LH* 648

Prayers:

Jesus Loves Me, Jesus Loves Me. *CGP*

Thank You, Jesus. *CK* 43

Lord, Bless the Little Children. *LFH* 36

Bible Words:

We love because He [God] first loved us. 1 John 4:19

Activities:

1. Make a scrapbook or mural of children from other lands (use pictures cut from magazines).

2. Color and cut out pictures of children from other lands (simple patterns may be used if desired).

3. Make a scrapbook or mural labeled "Who Loves Me?" Use pictures of parents, relatives, friends, etc.

4. Read: Pattibooks *Who Loves the Children?* and *Who Loves Patty?* (Wheaton, Ill.: Scripture Press). *Jesus, the Children's Friend* (New York: Abingdon Press).

5. Finger Plays: This Is My Mother. *CK* 43

Jesus Loves All Children. *FF* 22

B. Jesus Calls Children His Little Lambs
Bible Stories:

The Lost Sheep. Luke 15:1-7

Jesus Blesses the Children. Mark 10: 13-16; Luke 18:15-17

Anticipated Learnings:
Jesus wants all children to be His own and to be with Him in heaven.
Jesus wants me to be His child.

Songs:
I Am Jesus' Little Lamb. *LH* 648
God's a Father Kind and True. *LCSG* 13
God Is Near. *LCSG* 15

Prayers:
Jesus, Friend of Little Children. *CGP*
Jesus, Gentle Shepherd. *LFH* 6

Bible Words:
The Lord Is My Shepherd. Ps. 23:1
He [God] cares about you. 1 Peter 5:7

Activities:
1. Make a picture of a lamb, using cotton for the wool.
2. Draw a picture of your family.
3. Make a poster or scrapbook titled "Who Takes Care of Us?" Include parents, police, soldier, etc.
4. Begin a mission project.
5. Finger Plays: Jesus Loves All Children. *FF* 22
   Thank You, God. *FFF* 31

C. Jesus Helps Sick Children
Bible Stories:
The Nobleman's Son. John 4:46-53
Jairus' Daughter. Matt. 9:18-26

Anticipated Learnings:
Jesus helped a sick boy (girl).
Jesus will help me.

Songs:
'Tis Jesus Loves the Little Ones. *CGS* 18
Jesus Loves Me, This I Know. *LCSG* 16
I'm as Happy as Can Be. *LCSG* 17

Prayers:
Tender Jesus, Meek and Mild. *CGP*

Dear Jesus, Thou Art Always Good. *CK* 43
Jesus Loves Me, Jesus Loves Me. *CGP*
Lord Jesus, You Were Always Good. *LFH* 27

Bible Words:
God is good to the upright. Ps. 73:1
Call upon Me in the day of trouble; [and] I will deliver you. Ps. 50:15

Activities:
1. Make get-well cards for someone who is sick.
2. Say a prayer for a sick friend.
3. Make a poster of "Things to Keep Us Well."
4. Make a poster or scrapbook showing how Jesus uses people to help those who are sick (doctor, nurse, parents, pastor, etc.).
5. Make place mats and send them to a hospital.

D. Jesus Loves All Children Everywhere
Bible Stories:
Andrew Brings His Brother Peter to Jesus. John 1:35-42
The Little Slave Girl. 2 Kings 5:1-27

Anticipated Learnings:
Jesus loves everyone and wants them to be His children.
I can bring others to Jesus.

Songs:
Jesus Loves Children. *CGS* 76
Jesus Loves the Little Children. *LCSG* 75
Lord, Bless the Little Children. *LCSG* 77

Prayers:
Be Near Me, Lord Jesus. *CK* 44
Lord, Bless the Little Children. *LFH* 47

Bible Words:
Let us love one another. 1 John 4:7
Go into all the world and preach the Gospel. Mark 16:15
Be kind to one another. Eph. 4:32

Activities:

1. Begin or continue a mission project.
2. Make little banks and save coins for missions.
3. Make a poster or mural of children coming to Jesus.
4. Dramatize the Bible story.
5. Make a book titled "How I Can Help Jesus."
6. Finger Play: Come unto Me. *TBF* 30
7. Read: *Jesus, the Children's Friend* (New York: Abingdon Press). *Terry Finds a Lost Sheep* (St. Louis: Board for North American Missions, The Lutheran Church — Missouri Synod).

UNIT II
GOD CARES FOR HIS CHILDREN

Aim:

That the children may learn to know and appreciate God's protecting care for His people.

A. God Makes All Things

Bible Stories:

The Story of Creation. Gen. 1
God Creates Adam and Eve. Gen. 2

Anticipated Learnings:

God made all things.
God made me.
(First Article of Apostles' Creed — Creation)

Songs:

Who Made the Sky So Bright and Blue. *CGS* 66
Beautiful Savior. *LH* 657
God's Gifts to Me. *LCSG* 8
Oh, Who Can Make a Flower? *LCSG* 9
Thank You, Loving Father. *LCSG* 22

Prayers:

I Thank You, Jesus, for the Night. *LFH* 8

We Thank You, God, for Sunshine. *LFH* 36
God Made the Sun. *LFH* 40

Bible Words:

God created the heavens and the earth. Gen. 1:1
God created man in His own image. Gen. 1:27

Activities:

1. Make a "touch and feel" book. *CK* 45
2. Decorate a bulletin board with pictures of things God has made.
3. Collect leaves and flowers for a book.
4. Make a mural or frieze about creation.
5. Take a walk out of doors to see the things God has made.
6. Finger Plays: God's Creation. *FFF* 21
   I'm Glad God Gave Us Water. *FF* 12

B. God Watches Over His Children

Bible Stories:

The Baby Moses. Ex. 1:22 — 2:10
Joseph in Egypt. Gen. 39 — 41

Anticipated Learnings:

God took care of Moses and Joseph.
God will take care of me.
(First Article of Apostles' Creed — Preservation)

Songs:

God Is Near. *CGS* 30
'Tis Jesus Loves the Little Ones. *CGS* 18
God's a Father Kind and True. *LCSG* 13
God Is Always Near Me. *LCSG* 12
Now Thank We All Our God. *LH* 36

Prayers:

Heavenly Father, Hear My Prayer. *CGP*
Jesus, Tender Shepherd, Hear Me. *CGP*
Lord, Bless My Playmates. *CGP*

Bible Words:

I am with you and will keep you wherever you go. Gen. 28:15

God is with us. Is. 8:10

Activities:

1. Dramatize the story of Baby Moses.

2. Make a chart to show how God cares for us.

3. Draw a picture of Baby Moses in his basket or Joseph riding in the king's chariot.

4. Make a basket of paper; use a picture of a baby or a small doll to represent Moses.

5. Finger Plays: Little Baby Moses. *FFF* 22

   God Cares for All. *TBF* 51

C. God Sends His Angels to Watch His Children

Bible Stories:

Daniel and the Lions. Dan. 6
Three Men in the Fire. Dan. 3

Anticipated Learnings:

God took care of Daniel and the men.
God will take care of me.
(First Article of Apostles' Creed—Preservation)

Songs:

Dear Father in Heaven. *CGS* 35
I Am Jesus' Little Lamb. *LH* 648
God Is Near. *LCSG* 15
Jesus, Friend of Little Children. *LCSG* 19

Prayers:

Jesus Loves Me. *CGP*
Dear Father in Heaven. *CGP*
Dear Father Whom I Cannot See. *CGP*
Heavenly Father, Hear My Prayer. *LFH* 8

Bible Words:

I am with you and will keep you wherever you go. Gen. 28:15
I am with you always. Matt. 28:20

Activities:

1. Draw or paint pictures of angels.

2. Cut angels from colored paper. Paste on wings. Cover with artificial snow.

3. Make angels from plaster of paris.

4. Make paper and clay "stand-ups" of the story.

5. Draw a picture of the story.

6. Dramatize the story.

7. Make a diorama of the story.

D. God Gives Us Our Food

Bible Stories:

The Feeding of the 5,000. Matt. 14:13-21
Bread and Meat from Heaven. Ex. 16

Anticipated Learnings:

All our food comes from God.
Jesus fed many people.
Jesus will give me my food.
(First Article of Apostles' Creed—Preservation)

Songs:

Beautiful Savior. *LH* 657
Jesus Loves Me, This I Know. *CGS* 10
To God, Who Gives Us Daily Bread. *LCSG* 50
God, Bless This Food. *LCSG* 53

Prayers:

Come, Lord Jesus. *CGP*
Our Hands We Fold. *CGP*
Dear Jesus, Help Me. *CK* 48
We Thank You, Lord. *LFH* 24

Bible Words:

O give thanks to the Lord, for He is good. Ps. 118:1
The Lord will give what is good. Ps. 85:12

Activities:

1. Make a scrapbook called "Gifts from God."

2. Take a trip to a market or big store. Discuss God's abundant gifts.

3. Make a basket and fish out of paper and clay.

4. Make a chart showing a good meal.

5. Finger Plays: How Many Fish? *TBF* 29

  Loaves and Fish. *FFF* 27

UNIT III
JESUS HELPS MANY PEOPLE

Aim:

That the children may realize and appreciate more fully Jesus' wonderful love and His willingness to help them.

A. Jesus Helps People When They Need Him
Bible Stories:

The Wedding at Cana. John 2:1-11

The Captain and His Servant. Matt. 8:5-13

Anticipated Learnings:

Jesus helped people when they needed help.

Jesus will help me when I ask Him.

Songs:

Beautiful Savior. *LH* 657

Little Children, Pray to Jesus. *LCSG* 56

Jesus Loves Me, Jesus Loves Me. *CGS* 17

Prayers:

Jesus, Friend of Little Children. *CGP*

Blest Savior Dear. *LFH* 38

I Thank You, Dear Jesus. *CK* 47

Bible Words:

The Lord God helps me. Is. 50:7

The Lord has helped us. 1 Sam. 7:12

Activities:

1. Make posters of good things to eat, to wear, etc.

2. Plant window-box gardens and watch seeds grow.

3. Draw and color the waterpots, or make them of clay.

4. Make a picture of the captain talking to Jesus.

5. Ask children to pray sentence prayers asking Jesus' help.

B. Jesus Makes a Big Storm Stop
Bible Stories:

The Stilling of the Storm. Matt. 8:23-27; Luke 8:22-25

Jesus Walks on the Water. Matt. 14:22-33

Anticipated Learnings:

Jesus has power to help.

He helped the men who called on Him.

Jesus helps me when I need Him.

Songs:

I Am Trusting Thee, Lord Jesus. *LH* 428

I'm as Happy as Can Be. *LCSG* 17

God Is Near. *LCSG* 15

Prayers:

Help us, Dear Savior. *CK* 47

Be Near Me, Lord Jesus. *CGP*

Blest Savior Dear. *LFH* 38

Lord, Teach a Little Child to Pray. *LFH* 38

Bible Words:

God is mighty. Job 36:5

God has power to help. 2 Chron. 25:8

Activities:

1. Construct little boats of wood, paper, or soap.

2. Draw and color boats.

3. Finger-paint a picture of a storm.

4. Make a yarn picture of a boat on the Sea of Galilee.

5. Form a circle; ask each child to add one thought to the class's prayer.

C. Jesus Answers Prayer
Bible Stories:

The Daughter of Jairus. Matt. 9:18-19, 23-26

The Canaanite Woman. Matt. 15:21-28

Anticipated Learnings:

Jesus hears and answers the prayers of

those who believe in Him.
He will answer my prayers, too.

Songs:

Jesus Loves Me, Jesus Loves Me. *CGS* 17
Jesus Listens When I Pray. *LCSG* 36
Dear Lord Jesus, Hear My Prayer.
LCSG 42
What a Friend We Have in Jesus. *LH* 457

Prayers:

Help Us, Dear Jesus. *CK* 48
I Am Weak. *LFH* 28
Help Me Be Kind, Dear Jesus. *CK* 48

Bible Words:

God is my Helper. Ps. 54:4
Be kind to one another. Eph. 4:32

Activities:

1. Talk about prayer: how, where, for whom, for what, posture.
2. Make an illustrated booklet of familiar prayers.
3. Make cards or booklets for sick friends.
4. Make posters of "praying hands."
5. Finger Plays: Jesus Loves All Children. *FF* 22
   Prayer Time. *FFF* 31
   Thank You, God. *FFF* 31

D. Jesus Helps the Blind to See

Bible Stories:

Jesus and a Blind Man. Luke 18:35-43
Two Blind Men. Matt. 9:27-31

Anticipated Learnings:

The blind men believed that Jesus could help them.
I believe that Jesus can help me.
The blind man thanked Jesus for making him able to see.
I thank God for my eyes.

Songs:

Two Little Eyes. *CGS* 31

We Thank Thee, Heavenly Father. *CGS* 28

Prayers:

Jesus Loves Me, Jesus Loves Me. *CGP*
Jesus, Help My Eyes to See. *LFH* 31

Bible Words:

O give thanks to the Lord, for He is good. Ps. 118:1
It is good to give thanks to the Lord. Ps. 92:1

Activities:

1. Take a walk; note all the interesting things that can be seen.
2. Find pictures of pretty things; mount them on large sheets of paper.
3. Dramatize the story.
4. Ask the nurse to tell the children how to take care of their eyes.
5. Have children say short thank-you prayers for eyes, beautiful things, etc.

UNIT IV
GOD SENDS HIS SON

Aim:

That the children may know Jesus as God's greatest gift to the world.

A. God Promises a Savior from Sin

Bible Stories:

The First Sin. Gen. 3
Cain Kills His Brother. Gen. 4

Anticipated Learnings:

God promised a Savior from sin.
Jesus is my Savior.

Songs:

God Loves Me Dearly. *CGS* 56
Let Us All with Gladsome Voice. *LH* 97

Prayers:

Dear Jesus, You Have Promised Us Many Things. *CK* 49
Let Me Learn of Jesus, st. 2. *CGP*

Bible Words:

O give thanks to the Lord, for He is good. Ps. 118:1

God so loved the world that He gave His only Son. John 3:16

Activities:

1. Make a picture of Adam and Eve leaving the garden. Do not color skin of Adam and Eve, because we do not know what color it was.

2. Make a "temptation tree" (see *Religious Activities for Primary Children,* p. 11).

3. Ask children to illustrate different parts of the story; tape the illustrations together to make a "movie" or "TV" sequence

4. Finger Play: The First Family. *FFF* 22

B. God Keeps His Promises

Bible Stories:

The Annunciation. Luke 1:26-38

Mary Visits Elizabeth. Luke 1:39-56

Anticipated Learnings:

God promised to send His Son to be our helper.

The angel tells us that God keeps His promises.

Songs:

God Loves Me Dearly. *CGS* 56

Let Us All with Gladsome Voice. *LH* 97

Prayers:

Let Me Learn of Jesus, st. 2. *CGP*

Jesus, Friend of Little Children. *CGP*

Bible Words:

God is love. 1 John 4:8

With God nothing will be impossible. Luke 1:37

Activities:

1. Make angels for room decorations.

2. Prepare for Christmas by making tree decorations.

3. Make Christmas cards or place cards for hospitals.

4. Make (or buy) an Advent calendar. Use it each day.

5. Dramatize the angel's visit to Mary.

C. God Sends the Christmas Baby

Bible Story:

The Birth of Jesus. Luke 2:1-20

Anticipated Learnings:

God sent His Son Jesus to be our Savior from sin.

I love my Savior Jesus.

(Second Article of Apostles' Creed — Redemption)

Songs:

Away in a Manger. *CGS* 52

Silent Night. *LH* 646

In a Little Stable. *LCSG* 61

Our Little Hearts Are Glad Today. *LCSG* 67

Oh, Come, Let Us Adore Him. *LCSG* 64

Prayers:

Dear God, We Thank You. *CK* 49

Jesus, We Love You. *CK* 49

Be Near Me, Lord Jesus. *CGP*

Ah, Dearest Jesus, Holy Child. *CGS* 50, st. 4

Bible Words:

God so loved the world that He gave His only Son. John 3:16

God is love. 1 John 4:8

Activities:

1. Draw or paint pictures of the stable.

2. Make Christmas angels and ornaments.

3. Dramatize the story.

4. Trim a Christmas tree with ornaments.

5. Listen to Christmas records.

6. Sing Christmas carols with other classes.

7. Finger Plays: The Christmas Trees. *TBF* 38

   The Baby Jesus. *FFF* 25

8. Make a simple crèche.

9. Make a Christmas mural.

D. Little Jesus Gets Christmas Gifts

Bible Story:

The Coming of the Wise Men. Matt. 2:1-12

Anticipated Learnings:

Jesus came to save all people.

The Wise Men gave Jesus gifts because they loved Him.

I give Jesus my heart because I love Him.

Songs:

As Each Happy Christmas. *CGS* 49

God Loves Me Dearly. *CGS* 56

In a Little Stable. *LCSG* 61

From Heaven Above to Earth I Come. *LH* 85

Prayers:

What Can I Give Him? *CK* 50

Let Us All with Gladsome Voice. *CGS* 51, st. 4

Ah, Dearest Jesus, Holy Child. *CGS* 50, st. 4

Bible Words:

To us a Child is born, to us a Son is given. Is. 9:6

Activities:

1. Draw and paint a Christmas mural.

2. Make gifts for those we love.

3. Make or send gifts to underprivileged children; to residents of children's homes, homes for the mentally ill, homes for the aged, etc.

4. Finger Plays: How Jesus Was Born. *TBF* 36

   The Three Wise Men. *TBF* 37

   Baby Jesus. *FFF* 25

5. Dramatize the story.

6. Begin a mission project.

UNIT V
JESUS GROWS UP

Aim:

That the children may see in Jesus' holy life an example to follow, and that they may want to be more like Him.

A. Mary and Joseph Trust in God's Protection

Bible Story:

The Flight to Egypt. Matt. 2:13-23

Anticipated Learnings:

Mary and Joseph trusted in God.
God protected them.
My parents and I also trust in God.
(First Commandment)

Songs:

Jesus Loves Me, Jesus Loves Me. *CGS* 17
God Is Near. *CGS* 30
God Is Always Near Me. *LCSG* 12
God's a Father, Kind and True. *LCSG* 13
I'm as Happy as Can Be. *LCSG* 17

Prayers:

Dear Jesus, Help Me. *CK* 50
Heavenly Father, Hear My Prayer. *CGP*
Oh, Help Me, Lord, This Day to Be. *LFH* 5
O Blessed Lord, Protect Thou Me. *LFH* 10

Bible Words:

We have our hope set on the living God, who is the Savior of all men. 1 Tim. 4:10
Trust in the Lord with all your heart. Prov. 3:5

Activities:

1. Make a booklet showing God's protection at work, play, home, school, travel.

2. Finger Plays: The Boy Jesus. *FFF* 29
   A Happy Family. *TBF* 19

3. Make stand-up figures of clay (or paper) for a sand-table display.

4. Dramatize the story.

B. Jesus Goes to Church

Bible Stories:

Jesus in the Temple. Luke 2:41-52
Mary Listens to Jesus. Luke 10:38-42

Anticipated Learnings:

Jesus loved God's house and God's Word.
I love God's house and His Word, too.
(Third and Fourth Commandments)

Songs:

We Are in God's House Today. *CGS* 5
The Church Bell. *LCSG* 28
Sunday Morning Song. *LCSG* 31
In Our Church We Gladly Sing. *LCSG* 29

Prayers:

Lord Jesus, Bless the Pastor's Word. *CGP*
We Thank Thee, Heavenly Father. *LFH* 34
Heavenly Father, Please Help Me. *CK* 50

Bible Words:

This is . . . the house of God. Gen. 28:17
Children, obey your parents in the Lord. Eph. 6:1

Activities:

1. Draw and color church windows.
2. Visit the church; look at the windows, altar, pulpit.
3. Draw or paint pictures of objects in the church building.
4. Take a walk and look at the churches in the neighborhood.
5. Invite the pastor to tell about his work.
6. Read *When Jesus Was Twelve.*

C. Jesus Teaches About God's Love

Bible Stories:

The Sermon on the Mount (selections). Matt. 5—7.

Who Is Greatest in God's Kingdom? Matt. 18:1-4

Anticipated Learnings:

Jesus taught us that God is love.
We want to love one another.
(Fifth to Tenth Commandments)

Songs:

Beautiful Savior. *LH* 657
Teach Me to Love. *LCSG* 57
We Are Little Christian Children. *LCSG* 10

Prayers:

Dear God, Please Make Us Kind. *CK* 51
Lord, Bless My Playmates. *CGP*
Jesus, Friend of Little Children. *CGP*
Lord, Bless the Little Children. *LFH* 36

Bible Words:

Love one another. 1 John 4:7
Love your enemies. Matt. 5:44

Activities:

1. Make posters showing deeds of kindness being done to others.
2. Finger Plays: Two Little Hands. *TBF* 21
   We Can Help. *FFF* 58
3. Have children bring toys and books from home to share with the class for the week. Organize the materials into a "sharing corner."
4. Dramatize ways of helping and showing kindness to others.

D. Jesus Heals the Sick

Bible Stories:

The Paralyzed Man. Matt. 9:1-8; Mark 2:1-12

Jesus Heals a Sick Woman. Matt. 8:14-17

Anticipated Learnings:

Jesus wants to help everyone.
He will help me.

Songs:

I Am Trusting Thee, Lord Jesus. *LH* 428
Jesus Loves Me, This I Know. *CGS* 10
I'm as Happy as Can Be. *LCSG* 17
We Are Little Christian Children. *LCSG* 10

Prayers:

Jesus, Friend of Little Children. *CGP*
Be Near Me, Lord Jesus. *CGP*
Lord, Teach a Little Child to Pray. *LFH* 38

Bible Words:

Your sins are forgiven. Matt. 9:2
I [the Lord] will remember their sin no more. Jer. 31:34

Activities:

1. Make a house like the one in the first story. Use boxes, clay, or blocks.
2. Dramatize the story.
3. Illustrate the story, using crayon or paint.
4. Make get-well cards for sick friends.

UNIT VI
JESUS TAKES OUR SINS AWAY

Aim:

That the children may know Jesus as their personal Savior from sin.

A. People Hurt Jesus

Bible Story:

The Suffering and Death of Jesus. Matt. 26:14–27:66; Mark 14:10–15:47; Luke 22:1–23:56; John 13:1–19:42

Anticipated Learnings:

Jesus died to forgive the sins of the whole world.

Jesus died for me.

(Second Article of Apostles' Creed—Redemption)

Songs:

There Is a Green Hill Far Away. *CGS* 58

Let Me Learn of Jesus. *CGS* 57

Glory Be to Jesus. *LH* 158

Prayers:

Dear Jesus, You Are My Savior. *CK* 52

Jesus, Tender Savior. *LFH* 39

Bible Words:

He died for all. 2 Cor. 5:15

Christ died for our sins. 1 Cor. 15:3

Activities:

1. Make crosses of paper, clay, or wood; decorate them; use noodle letters to spell the name "Jesus."
2. Make picture frames of raffia or tongue depressors; insert pictures of Jesus.
3. Make a diorama of Calvary's hill or Joseph's garden and the tomb.
4. Make a simple Lenten mobile (cross, crown of thorns, nails, etc.).
5. Make a poster or mural titled "He Died for All."

B. Jesus Lives Again

Bible Story:

The Resurrection. Matt. 28:1-15; Mark 16:1-8; Luke 24:1-12; John 20:1-29.

Anticipated Learnings:

Jesus lives.

We will not stay dead.

We will live in heaven with Jesus.

(Second Article of Apostles' Creed—Redemption;

Third Article—Life Everlasting)

Songs:

On This Blessed Easter Day. *CGS* 61

O Happy Easter Morning. *CGS* 60

"Happy Easter" We Will Say. *LCSG* 72

Jesus Rose on Easter Day. *LCSG* 72

I Know that My Redeemer Lives. *LH* 200

Prayer:

Dear Father in Heaven. *CK* 53

Bible Words:

He has risen. Mark 16:6

Give thanks to Him [the Lord], bless His name! Ps. 100:4

Activities:

1. Make Easter crosses and Easter lilies.
2. Make a large cross of newspaper; decorate it with pictures of flowers from a seed catalog; mount the cross on the bulletin board.
3. Make an Easter morning diorama.
4. Make angels of paper or plaster of paris.
5. Make a picture of the first Easter.
6. Color eggs and put them in boxes or baskets decorated by the children; distribute to less fortunate children.

C. Jesus Shows Himself to His Friends

Bible Story:

Jesus on the Road to Emmaus. Luke 24:13-48; John 20:19-31

Anticipated Learnings:

Jesus showed Himself to His friends.

I cannot see Jesus, but I believe in Him because God has told me about Him in the Bible.

Songs:

Evening Shades Are Falling. *CGS* 40

This Is God's Word. *LCSG* 32

Prayers:

Thank You, Dear God. *CK* 54

Let Me Learn of Jesus. *CGP*

We Thank Thee, Heavenly Father. *LFH* 34

Bible Words:

The Lord is risen indeed! Luke 24:34

Believe in the Lord Jesus, and you will be saved. Acts 16:31

Activities:

1. Have the children bring Bibles or Bible story books to school. Emphasize that the Bible is God's Word. Read stories from the books the children bring.

2. Make Bible verse posters of favorite Bible passages. Use alphabet noodles or cereal "Alphabits."

D. Jesus Goes Home to Heaven

Bible Story:

The Ascension. Matt. 28:16-20; Luke 24:50-53; Acts 1:6-11

Anticipated Learnings:

Heaven is Jesus' home.

I want to go to heaven.

Jesus will take me there.

Songs:

God Is Near. *CGS* 30

Jesus Loves Me, This I Know. *CGS* 10

Oh, Help Me, Lord. *LCSG* 39

Jesus, Keep Me All Day Long. *LCSG* 41

Draw Us to Thee. *LH* 215

Prayers:

Jesus, Tender Shepherd, Hear Me, st. 3. *CGP*

Jesus, Friend of Little Children. *CGP*

Bible Words:

I am with you always. Matt. 28:20

Activities:

1. Make a picture of the Ascension; use cotton for the clouds.

2. Make a prayer book using prayers the children have learned.

3. Talk about prayer.

4. Make a mural of the Lenten and Easter stories.

UNIT VII
JESUS TEACHES US

Aim:

That the children may know some of Jesus' teachings and use them to guide their lives

A. God's Children Help Others

Bible Stories:

The Good Samaritan. Luke 10:29-37

Jesus Accepts Zacchaeus. Luke 19:1-10

Anticipated Learnings:

God's people are kind and helpful to others.

I want to show my love to God by being kind and helpful to others. (Fourth to Tenth Commandments)

Songs:

I Want to Live for Jesus. *CGS* 22

I Want to Be a Helper. *LCSG* 60

Holy Spirit, Give Us. *LCSG* 38

Prayers:

Help Me to Do the Things I Should. *CK* 57

Jesus, Friend of Little Children. *CGP*

Jesus, Lead Me Day by Day. *LFH* 8

Bible Words:

Be kind to one another. Eph. 4:32

Let us love one another. 1 John 4:7

Activities:

1. Dramatize the story.

2. Draw pictures showing how the priest, the Levite, and the Samaritan acted when they saw the wounded traveler.

3. Make a poster showing how we can be kind and helpful to others.

4. Have the children suggest and dramatize ways to be helpful to others.

5. Find pictures of children doing good deeds.

6. Help some needy family in the community, or pack boxes for the Junior Red Cross.

B. Jesus Forgives Sins

Bible Stories:

The Lost Son. Luke 15:11-32
The Lost Sheep. Luke 15:3-7

Anticipated Learnings:

Jesus loves sinners and forgives them.
Jesus loves me and forgives me.
(Second Article of Apostles' Creed — Redemption;
Third Article — Forgiveness)

Songs:

Let Me Learn of Jesus. *CGS* 57
Oh, How I Love Jesus. *LCSG* 21
We Thank You, Loving Father. *LCSG* 24

Prayer:

I Am So Happy to Know that You Love Me. *CK* 55

Bible Words:

I am sorry for my sin. Ps. 38:18
God, be merciful to me a sinner! Luke 18:13

Activities:

1. Talk about God's Commandments.

2. Make pictures or a poster showing how God's Commandments are broken every day (children fighting, disobeying parents, etc.).

3. Make a sheep, using cotton for wool.

4. Have the children suggest and dramatize ways of solving everyday problems in a God-pleasing manner.

5. Finger Play: The Lost Sheep. *FFF* 28

C. God's Children Gladly Hear His Word

Bible Stories:

Mary Listens to Jesus. Luke 10:38-42

Jesus in the Temple. Luke 2:41-52

Anticipated Learnings:

Mary learned much about Jesus.
I want to learn about Jesus, too.
(Third Commandment)

Songs:

We Are in God's House Today. *CGS* 5
The Best Book of All. *LCSG* 35
Sunday Morning Song. *LCSG* 31
Holy Bible, God's Own Word. *LCSG* 33

Prayers:

Dear Jesus, Help Me. *CK* 56
Lord Jesus, Bless the Pastor's Word. *CGP*
We Thank Thee, Heavenly Father. *LFH* 34

Bible Words:

Blessed . . . are those who hear the Word of God and keep it! Luke 11:28
I was glad when they said to me, "Let us go to the house of the Lord!" Ps. 122:1

Activities:

1. Let the children handle the Bible and Bible story books.

2. Visit the church; look at its parts, furnishings, etc.

3. Make a church; use cartons and boxes.

4. Make scrolls; print favorite Bible verses on them.

5. Draw or paint pictures of people going to church.

6. Make a "church book"; show different parts of the church (altar, pulpit, etc.).

D. Jesus Teaches Us to Pray

Bible Stories:

The Lord's Prayer. Luke 11:1-4; Matt. 6:5-15
Two Men Pray. Luke 18:9-14

Anticipated Learnings:

Jesus wants us to pray.
Jesus shows us how to pray.

I will pray to Jesus.
(Third Commandment)

Songs:
Let Me Learn of Jesus. *CGS* 57
Jesus Listens When I Pray. *LCSG* 36
Little Children, Pray to Jesus. *LCSG* 56
Teach Me to Love. *LCSG* 57
What a Friend We Have in Jesus. *LH* 457

Prayers:
See *CK* 45, 46
Lord, Teach a Little Child to Pray. *CGP*

Bible Words:
Lord, teach us to pray. Luke 11:1
The Lord accepts my prayer. Ps. 6:9

Activities:
1. Make a prayer book; include prayers composed by the class.
2. Draw or paint pictures to illustrate the petitions of the Lord's Prayer.
3. Make a poster showing times to pray (mealtime, bedtime, etc.).
4. Have a child speak or lead the table prayer for the snack period.
5. Form a circle; have each child (or several children) add a thought to the prayer for the day.

UNIT VIII
GOD'S CHILDREN LOVE JESUS

Aim:
That the children may learn to live a God-pleasing life for the Savior's sake.

A. God's Children Praise Jesus
Bible Stories:
Jesus Enters Jerusalem. Matt. 21:1-11; Mark 11:1-11; Luke 19:29-40
The Wise Men Worship Jesus. Matt. 2:1-12

Anticipated Learnings:
The little children and adults worshiped Jesus.

I will worship Jesus too.

Songs:
I Want to Live for Jesus. *CGS* 22
My Best Friend Is Jesus. *LCSG* 20
In Our Church We Gladly Sing. *LCSG* 29
Praise God, from Whom All Blessings Flow. *LH* 644
Praise Him, Praise Him. *CGS* 70

Prayers:
Dear Jesus, Help Me to Love You More. *CK* 56
May You Live to Know and Fear God. *LFH* 48

Bible Words:
Sing praises to God! Ps. 47:6
O give thanks to the Lord, for He is good. Ps. 118:1

Activities:
1. Review songs learned so far.
2. Arrange a "singing time" with another grade.
3. Make palm branches out of crepe or construction paper.
4. Sing a special song in a church or chapel service.
5. Make a book of favorite songs.
6. Make a sand-table picture of the story.

B. God's Children Serve Him
Bible Stories:
The Widow's Coins. Mark 12:41-44; Luke 21:1-4
God Calls Moses to Serve Him. Ex. 3 and 4

Anticipated Learnings:
God gives me everything I need.
I will show my thanks to God.
I will serve God with my gifts.

Songs:
Offering. *CGS* 12
Offering Prayer. *CGS* 14
Our Hands We Fold. *LCSG* 80

Since My Heavenly Father. *LCSG* 80

Prayers:

Savior, Use the Gift I Lay. *CGP*

Lord, We Bring Our Offering. *LFH* 35

Jesus, Bless the Gifts We Bring Thee.
LFH 33

Bible Words:

If a man loves Me, he will keep My Word.
John 14:23

Activities:

1. Make little banks, and save coins for missions or charitable purposes.

2. Make scrapbook or poster showing how we can serve Jesus.

3. Invite the pastor or one of the teachers to tell about his work.

4. Talk about and find pictures of ways to serve Jesus in church (choir, usher, etc.).

C. God's Children Show Love to Others

Bible Stories:

David and Jonathan. 1 Sam. 18 – 20

Ruth and Naomi. Ruth 1

Anticipated Learnings:

God's Bible people helped each other.

I love and trust God.

I want to show my love for God by loving others.

(Fourth to Tenth Commandments)

Songs:

I Want to Live for Jesus. *CGS* 22

We Are Little Christian Children. *LCSG* 10

I Want to Be a Helper. *LCSG* 60

Prayers:

Lord, Bless My Playmates. *CGP*

Teach Me to Love. *LFH* 7

Help Me to Do the Things I Should.
LFH 8

May My Sins Be All Forgiven. *LFH* 16

Bible Words:

Through love be servants of one another.
Gal. 5:13

Activities:

1. Tell stories and draw pictures of how children can help other people.

2. Talk about the Commandments that tell us how to help our friends and neighbors.

3. Make a booklet called "Things I Can Do to Help."

4. Dramatize ways to help our parents and friends.

D. God's Children Do God's Will

Bible Stories:

The Boy Joseph. Gen. 37 – 40

Samuel and Eli. 1 Sam. 1 – 4

Anticipated Learnings:

God gives us rules to obey.

Joseph obeyed God's rules.

I will try to obey God's rules.

(Ten Commandments)

Songs:

Two Little Eyes. *CGS* 31

My Father and My Mother. *LCSG* 54

My Father and My Mother Dear. *CGS* 34

Prayers:

Heavenly Father, Please Help Me. *CK* 57

Dear Father in Heaven. *CGP*

Bible Words:

You shall do what is right and good in the sight of the Lord. Deut. 6:18

Activities:

1. Draw or paint Joseph's coat of many colors.

2. Talk about the Fourth Commandment.

3. Make a booklet or poster titled, "I Help My Parents."

UNIT IX

PEOPLE WHO LOVED GOD

Aim:

That the children may know some of

God's heroes of faith and seek in Christ to imitate their virtues.

A. Men of Faith

Bible Stories:

Abraham, the Man of Faith. Gen. 12:1-5; 15:1-6: 18:1-15; 21:1-7

Jacob's Wonderful Dream. Gen. 27 and 28

Anticipated Learnings:

Abraham believed in God.

I will believe like Abraham.

(First Commandment; First Article of Apostles' Creed)

Songs:

I Am Trusting Thee, Lord Jesus. *LH* 428

I Believe in God. *LCSG* 12

My Best Friend Is Jesus. *LCSG* 20

Oh, How I Love Jesus. *LCSG* 21

Prayers:

Dear Father in Heaven. *CK* 57

Jesus Loves Me, Jesus Loves Me. *CGP*

Bible Words:

I will indeed bless you. Gen. 22:17

Activities:

1. Begin a book or mural titled "Men of God" or "Bible Heroes."
2. Review the Bible words and songs learned during the year.
3. Make a tent like Abraham's out of construction paper.
4. Dramatize Abraham's moving day.
5. Make a picture of Jacob's dream.

B. Men of Trust

Bible Stories:

God Feeds Elijah. 1 Kings 16:29 — 17:24

Noah and the Great Flood. Gen. 6 — 9

Anticipated Learnings:

Elijah trusted God to help him.

I will trust God too.

(First Commandment; First Article of Apostles' Creed)

Songs:

Beautiful Savior. *LH* 657

God Is Always Near Me. *LCSG* 12

God Is Near. *LCSG* 15

Jesus Loves Me, This I Know. *CGS* 10

Prayers:

Dear Jesus, Please Help Me. *CK* 58

Jesus, Tender Shepherd, Hear Me. *CGP*

Bible Words:

I trust in the Lord. Ps. 31:6

Activities:

1. Add to the book or mural titled "Men of God" or "Bible Heroes."
2. Draw pictures of birds, the food, and the brook in the Elijah story.
3. Make posters showing "how God cares for me."
4. Make Noah's ark and animals (see *Religious Activities for Primary Children*, p. 13).

C. Mighty Preachers

Bible Stories:

The Story of Pentecost. Acts 2

Paul and Silas in Prison. Acts 16:16-34

Anticipated Learnings:

Paul worked for Jesus.

I will work for Jesus too.

(Third Article of Apostles' Creed)

Songs:

Holy Spirit, Hear Us. *LH* 229

Jesus Loves the Little Children. *LCSG* 75

We Bring to You Our Love-Gifts. *LCSG* 79

Prayers:

Lord, Let Your Holy Spirit Come into My Heart. *CK* 58

Dear Lord, Will You Not Help Us? *LFH* 47

Lord, Bless the Little Children. *LFH* 47

Bible Words:

Teach me to do Thy will, for Thou art my God! Ps. 143:10

Activities:

1. Let the children tell some of the Bible stories they have heard this year.

2. Dramatize some of the Bible stories learned.

3. Make a series of pictures showing Paul preaching, Paul in prison, etc.

4. Review memory work learned.

D. Great Missionaries

Bible Stories:

Paul Becomes a Missionary. Acts 8:1-4; 9:1-30

Philip and the Ethiopian. Acts 8:26-39

Anticipated Learnings:

The apostle Paul loved Jesus and worked for Him.

I love Jesus and I will work for Him too.

Songs:

Jesus Loves Me, This I Know. *CGS* 10

Dear Savior, Bless the Children. *LCSG* 73

Little Children, Pray to Jesus. *LCSG* 56

Prayers:

Dear Heavenly Father. *CK* 58

Jesus, Friend of Little Children. *CGP*

Lord, Teach a Little Child to Pray. *CGP*

Dear Savior, Bless the Children. *LFH* 34

Bible Words:

Go into all the world and preach the Gospel. Mark 16:15

Activities:

1. Add to the book or mural titled "Men of God" or "Bible Heroes."

2. Have children bring in names of children who may be won during the summer for Sunday school, vacation Bible school, or Christian elementary school.

3. Choose a mission project and make a bank for gathering coins.

4. Make a diorama of the story.

In all activities provide the children with many and varied opportunities for self-expression, especially to express their love for others and to share the "Good News" of God's love in Christ.

5. Growing Through Social Experiences

Bless me, O Lord, that I may
Show Your boys and girls the way
That leads to You.

Help me, O Lord, that I may
Teach their tiny lips to pray
Their prayers to You.

HUMAN RELATIONS
NEED TO BE IMPROVED

There is a growing concern for the improvement of human relations. The tragic experiences of conflict and the struggles for peace have highlighted the necessity for establishing a better understanding among people. Improved human relations begin with individuals, and since education is concerned first of all with the improvement of individuals, educational thought and practice is stressing the importance of proper human relations more and more.

One of the great values in a Christian democracy lies in the development of a strong, cooperative personality. This development is brought about by constructive relations with other people and groups and by the right relation between the individual and God. This type of growth should be one of the main objectives in a Christian kindergarten.

THE CHRISTIAN KINDERGARTEN CAN
PROVIDE A WHOLESOME CHRISTIAN
INFLUENCE

We, as Christian teachers, have the means to bring about proper social adjustment of the individual. We have, above all, the Word of God with its perfect directives for Christian child training. The greatest truths in child psychology are to be found in the teachings of Jesus Christ.

All learning situations should be directed toward this goal of socialization and Christian living. The social growth of the child is essential for his well-being and cannot be separated from the development of the child's total personality. The child is influenced by all things in his environment, and he reacts to them as whole person. Teachers in Christian kindergartens have the responsibility of providing an environment which exerts a wholesome Christian influence.

THE PURPOSE OF
A SOCIAL STUDIES PROGRAM

The purpose of a social studies program should be to give the children a chance to understand the complex world into which God has placed them, and then to build on this knowledge and experience to gain a greater understanding of other people and their cultures. It should build—

1. Worthwhile social understandings

2. Desirable attitudes toward others

3. Positive Christian ways of behavior

THE SOCIAL STUDIES CURRICULUM

A comprehensive, functional, and well-organized program should deal with all the basic human activities in which man is engaged. Each should be treated according to its own particular importance in the life and interest of the kindergarten child. When learning about the problems of the world and the needs of mankind, an orderly sequence should be kept in mind, but not necessarily rigidly adhered to.

Although it may be advisable to start with familiar surroundings—home, family, friends—today's kindergarten children live in an expanded world and come into daily contact with events that take place all over the world. They actively live in an atomic- and space-conscious atmosphere. Therefore, introduction of certain problems cannot be postponed. Concepts, attitudes, and values are built in children at a very early age.

New insights into the young child's potential indicate that cognitive learnings should not be withheld as they grow in this fast-changing culture. A learning experience today should provide the correct conceptual base for significant later experiences. However, ideas must still be kept simple enough for the child to grasp and make his own. These simple concepts will then be a foundation for more complex future learnings in a type of "spiral" approach.

It has been said that a kindergarten program is essentially a social studies program. This in a sense is true.

A well-planned unit of work will utilize all phases of activity: planning together, sharing of experiences through language, the natural sciences, dramatization, construction, creating, singing, listening, taking trips, and many others. All these activities will help the children grow intellectually as well as lead them into desirable patterns of behavior.

Good content material will accelerate progress in thinking and reasoning. Teachers must become skillful in identifying meaningful and challenging materials that will actively involve the children in exploring, manipulating, and evaluating. Children of today are aware of geography, history, and economics and welcome opportunities for concrete experiences. The teacher must be acquainted with the various bodies of knowledge from which "content learning" can be drawn. She will learn to be a master in putting this in a framework children will enjoy.

The choice of a unit may come out of the free discussions of the children, a friendly walk in the neighborhood, a trip, a filmstrip, or a story; but it can also be preplanned by the teacher.

In her planning the teacher will provide experiences and activities for all her pupils according to their rate of growth. One group of children may be able to construct things while another may paint or draw. Some children may be happy just to observe or to cut out pictures, but all will feel that they belong to the working group. Identical achievement in all areas of learning cannot be expected from each child in the group, yet each child should be expected to do his or her best according to the talents God has given and the stage of development at which the child has arrived.

When planning units of study, it is well to keep definite objectives in mind, refer to them occasionally, and then, at the end of the unit, make an evaluation of content growth and of social Christian living and learning.

OBJECTIVES TO BE KEPT IN MIND

1. To develop in the children the ability to work well with others (Christian behavior).

2. To teach them to take turns graciously and to respect the rights and opinions of those working with them.

3. To teach them to obey and respect group rules.

4. To help them learn to listen to other friends' suggestions and be willing to try them.

5. To show them how they can help others and share ideas and properties with them.

6. To help them grow in appreciation of the finer things in life.

7. To help them broaden their knowledge and deepen their understanding.

8. To teach them tolerance and love for others.

9. To help them grow in appreciation of God's great mercy and of the blessings He freely gives.

It is wise for the teacher to:

1. Try to get an overview of the whole unit.

2. Make plans as to how she is going to introduce it and what activities she will use.

3. List and study appropriate books and pamphlets and other source materials for the needed factual information.

4. Prepare an organized plan of procedure.

5. Prepare for a good start with proper motivation—create an interest.

When the unit is completed, the teacher may ask herself:

1. Did we reach our desired goals?

2. Was there growth on the part of the children?

3. Did all the children participate?

4. Did they enjoy their work and play?

5. Was Christian behavior noticeable?

After her evaluation she may wish to culminate the unit by asking the parents or other students to come in for a visit and see the various things the children have made.

EXPANDING UNITS

With the children's various backgrounds one can expect a spread of interests. Since *home and family* is common to all children, however, it is a sound choice for a beginning.

Other units with high interests are:

1. The school and church

2. Animals and their young
   a. Zoo
   b. Circus

3. A visit to
   a. A police station
   b. A firehouse
   c. An airport

4. People and their work
   a. Bus driver
   b. Doctor, etc.

5. Other people in the world

6. Buying at stores

7. How ships help us

8. Space travel

GET ACQUAINTED
WITH THE PUPILS FIRST

Perhaps at the beginning of the year, a teacher may wish to spend some time in getting acquainted with her pupils as individuals before planning a larger unit of study. She may wish to build a short unit to aid in getting better acquainted while she listens, observes, and learns. A particular child may have been to a circus or a fair, or perhaps one has just had an interesting trip. Any item of interest to which the group reacts is a good starting point for the "Getting Acquainted" unit.

During the first few days, while the short unit is in progress, the teacher uses every opportunity to study the interests and characteristics of each child in her group. She observes the children at play, watching for traits of selfishness, overaggressiveness, extreme shyness, and other negative behavior, as well as for desirable traits. She watches closely to see how far each child has matured in all the phases of growth, so that she can set up standards of achievement that will be commensurate with each child's personal growth pattern.

She will also, through discussions and through watching the children's behavior during the activity periods, learn to know the common experiences and the main interests of her children.

THE HOME AND FAMILY

After a few days of becoming acquainted, the children will begin to realize that we are all in God's family and that we also have a school family. They are proud of their own families and will be anxious to share their home experiences. They will gradually realize that God has planned families and expects each child to take his place in his particular family and to help make his home a happy place in which to live.

THE SCHOOL

After working through the unit on the home and family, the children have become fairly well acquainted. Perhaps they have started to visit one another in their homes, and perhaps the teacher has also had the opportunity to visit the children. At this time they are ready to explore their new surroundings. They will be interested in seeing who works in the school building and what these people do. A trip to the boiler room, to the other classrooms, to the church, and to the pastor's study are worthwhile experiences for the children. During this time the teacher will continue to observe and guide the children's behavior in new surroundings and new situations.

An indexed notebook with a page for each child is an excellent way to keep a running record of the child's reactions and achievements.

THE DEVELOPMENT OF OTHER UNITS

Some units will develop out of suggestions made by the children or from some of their personal experiences. A child may have returned from a trip with his parents, or a group may have been to the circus. A foreign child may have joined the school family, or a historical event may be in the making. Some units may be of short duration, depending on the interest and the maturity of the group. While planning these units, a teacher will want to set up "centers of interest" around the room to which the children may go for added information. Filmstrips, pictures, books, and collections always add interest.

Children tend to be interested in an overview of their total environment in abbreviated ways, rather than centering their interest on long-time values. For that reason units should not be too long.

TOPICS FOR SHORT UNITS

Science topics, weather changes, seasonal observations, and festivals or holidays provide suitable topics for short units. The following special events could be celebrated:

Halloween—with pumpkins and black cats

Reformation Day—churches—Luther as a boy

Thanksgiving—Pilgrims and Indians

Christmas—with its many activities

Birthdays of the children—parties or treats

Valentine Day—with a post office

Easter—crosses, eggs, and bunnies

May Day—a basket for mother

Memorial Day—flags, parades

Mother's Day—gifts for mother

Father's Day—gifts for father

Famous Men—the flag—the log cabin

UN Week—display and flags

Library Week—books, story time

Special days for ethnic groups

Some of these should be very short, perhaps lasting only a day or two, while others can be used as topics for units around which longer units can be planned.

CHRISTMAS

Christmas with its many activities serves as a fascinating and extensive unit. Naturally the story of the Christ Child is the center of interest around which related things — trees, ornaments, toys, songs, games, and all kinds of craft activities — are correlated.

Little children are also interested in Christmas in other lands. The different ways in which children of other countries celebrate fascinates them and assists in building understanding of and tolerance for other people.

THE FARM, PETS

A trip to a nearby farm may be a starting point for an extensive farm unit, or it may suggest the bringing of pets to school for a day or so. If this is attempted, a suitable place should be provided for the pets so that they will not suffer unduly by the visit. Some children will prefer to bring their stuffed toys and pets in place of real ones. Related activities such as making butter, baking bread, or perhaps planting a garden provide ideal opportunities for content and appreciation growth.

INDIANS

Indians with drums, tents, canoes, and all the related activities seem to be favorites with kindergarten children, and a unit built around them serves as a basis for a program for the mothers or for an assembly program. Such a unit correlates well with art and music.

THE HOME AND FAMILY
(Sample Unit)

The study of *The Home and Family* as a starting unit is presented in outline form and may serve as a pattern for other units.

During the entire unit it is well to keep specific objectives in mind, so that the purpose of the unit is not lost. These objectives must be clear in the mind of the teacher; the children, too, should be taught to be aware of the purposes of the unit. The objectives are not referred to in a formal academic manner but are, nevertheless, present in the minds and attitudes of the participants.

THE TEACHER'S OBJECTIVES

1. An understanding of Christian home life.

2. An application of principles of Christian living.

3. An appreciation and knowledge of God-fearing homes mentioned in the Bible.

4. A demonstration of a Christian pupil-teacher relationship; also of Christian teacher-parent relationship.

5. A clear conception of the major goals as they affect the lives of the children.

THE CHILDREN'S OBJECTIVES

1. A realization that God has made the family, and that He wants its members to live together as happy, useful, Christian people.

2. An appreciation of family life and a sense of gratitude for their own home and family.

3. A willingness to assume small responsibilities in the home.

4. An awareness of the dependence on others who help make home life comfortable (milkman, grocer, doctor, pastor, farmer, baker, fireman, nurse).

5. A realization that through these helpers we receive God's gifts.

6. An appreciation of different types of homes.

7. A feeling of dependence on God for all needs and a thankful heart for all His blessings.

8. A feeling of respect and sincere love for members of the family (father, mother, grandparents, sisters, and brothers).

9. An understanding of the roles and activities of the family members.

10. A realization that a home must be furnished and maintained.

STARTING THE UNIT

The following suggestions may be useful in finding an approach to the study of family life.

1. Conversation about home activities and family life.

2. A natural transition from the love and protection of God to that of parents.

3. An excursion to see the building of a new home in the community.

4. The dollhouse and activities in the room.

5. A story, song, or poem about home activities.

6. Visitors that come to the home (company).

7. Brothers and sisters who stay at home.

8. Dramatic play that is related to home life (cooking, ironing, washing, dusting, sweeping).

9. Playing with blocks and constructing houses.

10. Moving of a child from one house to another.

After interest has been created and a plan of action is clear in the mind of the teacher, she will have to decide on her procedure. She may show a filmstrip of homes and their helpers, or she may have the children gather pictures of family groups in various activities: perhaps traveling, going on a picnic, going to church, giving a party.

The teacher may also wish to invite the parents and little brothers and sisters to visit school; she may ask the children to draw pictures of their family; she may read stories of family life; she may have the children tell interesting stories about their home life or bring actual photographs to school.

UNIT OUTLINE

I. LEARNING ABOUT HOMES AND FAMILY MEMBERS

A. General Activities

1. Find out where the children live.
   a. By conversations.
   b. By taking walks.

2. Find out in what kind of homes the children live.
   a. One-story homes.
   b. Two-story.
   c. Apartment houses.
   d. Ranch homes.
   e. Condominiums.
   f. Mobile homes.

3. Find out how the children help in their homes.
   a. Talk about what they do.
   b. Have them draw pictures of how they help.
   c. Dramatize the various activities.

4. Find out what other members of the family do.
   a. Where does father work?
   b. Where does mother work?
   c. What do the sisters and brothers do?

5. Learn poems and sing songs about the family and the home.
   a. Read poems to the children; also have them memorize simple verses.
   b. Sing songs and act them out.
6. Encourage family devotion and prayers in the family.
   a. Teach some simple prayers.
   b. Tell the children how their parents can read stories about Jesus to them.
7. Talk about making a dollhouse or a playhouse at school.
   a. Materials—blocks, orange crate, boxes.
   b. Space available in the room.
   c. Furnishings.

B. Arts and Crafts Activities

1. Depict "My House," "My Family," "My Room," "My Pets" in the various art media.
2. Make a box-type movie with self-made portraits.

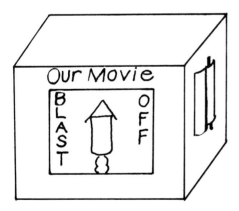

3. Make use of dramatic play and role playing.
4. Make a frieze on long brown wrapping paper. Paste or paint the pictures.

5. Make a scrapbook of the children's home and the members of the family. Cut pictures from magazines.
6. Prepare a bulletin board with appropriate displays.

C. Instructional Activities

1. Talk about homes and families: what our fathers and mothers do, our pets, how we help, fun at home, etc.
2. Study books about home and family, furniture, and related subjects.
3. Learn basic concepts from books, slides, films, tapes, and recordings.
4. Visit stores, a house being built, a garden, or a pet shop.

II. STUDYING ABOUT THINGS USED IN THE HOME

A. General Activities

1. Talk about the different kinds of foods.
   a. Milk.
   b. Meat.
   c. Vegetables.
   d. Fruits.
2. Find out where food comes from.
   a. Take a trip to the grocery store.
   b. Go to a dairy or a farm.
   c. Have the milkman or the butcher come in and talk to the children.
3. Learn about the value of food.
   a. How it helps us grow.
   b. The price of food.
   c. How we preserve it.
   d. Never to waste it.
   e. Prepare some if possible. (Roll out some cookie dough, and let the children cut their own cookies with cookie cutters. Bake them at school or at home.)

4. Observe how God gives us all we need.
   a. How He lets plants grow.
   b. How animals serve mankind.
   c. How He provides all we need. (Refer here to the story of *Jesus Feeding the Five Thousand.*)

5. Study the need for clothing.
   a. Summer clothing.
   b. Winter clothing.

6. Learn about the different kinds of materials.
   a. What they are.
   b. Where they come from.
   c. How we use them.

7. Study about the utilities.
   a. Heating of homes.
   b. Electricity.
   c. Gas.
   d. Water.

8. Stress health and safety in the home.
   a. Good habits of eating, sleeping, and cleanliness.
   b. Dangers (matches, gas, and electricity).
   c. Precautions (straight rugs, good lights).
   d. Angel protection.

B. Art Activities

1. Children enjoy tearing colored paper to represent the different vegetables and fruits. Some of the easiest to tear out are tomatoes, carrots, squash, turnips, oranges, apples, pumpkins, and bananas.

2. Make posters of food.
   a. A good breakfast.
   b. A good lunch or dinner.
   c. Foods that grow under the ground.

d. Foods we buy.

3. Do some creative painting of vegetables and fruits.

4. Make and dress dolls.
   a. Dress them with different kinds of materials.
   b. Clothespin dolls can easily be dressed with simple clothes.
   c. Make an outline pattern of a girl or a boy and cut out the suit or dress leaving the outline. Paste the materials the child selects in the back, so that the dress or suit will show on the front. Paste a piece of paper over the material to keep it firm. Let the child color the doll's face, hair, socks, and shoes. Various materials may be used: Cotton, silk, wool, linen.

5. Make posters of clothes worn by boys, clothes worn by girls, clothes for winter, clothes for summer.

6. Draw and color pictures of some of the good things God gives us. Make posters for the room or booklets to take home.

7. Make papier-mâché dolls or vegetables.

cut on dotted line.

8. Make and dramatize with puppets.

9. Illustrate stories you have read or told to the children.

C. Culminating Activities

1. Invite the mothers in to see the "movie" and other activities.

2. Invite some of the other grades in to see the "movie" or some dramatic play.

3. Make a story chart about the "movie." Get the thoughts from the children and write it on large paper.

4. Plan an exhibit of your work—the frieze, the prayer book, the drawings, the houses, etc.

5. Learn and sing appropriate songs about home and family, and share them with other schoolmates.

6. Have a storytime in which the children tell their favorite stories about homes. Bring in the homelife of Bible times.

Prayers for Home and Family

Come, Lord Jesus, be our Guest,
And let Thy gifts to us be blest. Amen.

We thank You for the world so sweet,
We thank You for the food we eat,
We thank You for the birds that sing,
We thank You, God, for everything. Amen.

Jesus, bless my mother,
Bless my daddy, too.
Make our happy family
Love and honor You.

Our hands we fold,
Our heads we bow;
For food and drink
We thank Thee now.

When I go to bed at night,
Mother dear turns out the light.

Then I know that I'm all right,
For Jesus watches me.

When my night of rest is done,
God turns on His light, the sun.
Then I work and have my fun,
For Jesus watches me.

Bless my mommy,
Jesus dear.
Keep Your angels
Always near.

Bless my daddy
Through the day.
Keep all danger
Far away.

Let us all Your
Children be,
Bless our whole
Dear family.

Forgive me, God, for being bad;
I'm sorry that I made You sad.
Help me to love You and be good,
And try to do the things I should.
Help me obey my parents dear,
Who teach me You are always near
To guide me through each happy day.
And lead me on the heavenly way.

I love you, Mother,
And Jesus does too.
I pray for His blessing
On all that you do.

God bless you, Daddy,
While you're away,
And bless and keep you
All through the day.

I love you, Mother,
Oh, so well—
No words of mine
Can ever tell.

You always are
So good to me;

A good child I
Will try to be.

Be with us on our homeward way.
Protect and guide us, Lord, we pray.
Look down upon us from Thy throne,
And let us all come safely home. Amen.

God made the sun,
And God made the tree.
God made the mountains,
And God made me.

I thank You, O God,
For the sun and the tree,
For making the mountains,
And for making me.

A Finger Play

Ten little men to market go!
Thumbkins go to buy some wheat;
Pointers go to buy some meat;
Tall men go to carry back
Great big bundles in their sack;
Ring men go to buy some silk;
Babies go to buy some milk;
Mother and Daddy go with me
To shop for our dear family.

This little hand
Some work can do.
And it can write,
"I love you," too.

The Family

We are a happy family,
A happy home have we,
With father and with mother,
Who love us tenderly.
The dear Lord Jesus loves us,
He loves us all, you see,
And He makes all His children
A happy family.

We are a happy family,
A happy home have we,
With sisters and with brothers,
Who love us tenderly.
Our heavenly Father loves us,
He loves us all, you see,
And He makes all His children
A happy family.*

* *Children's Hymnal and Service Book.* Philadelphia:
United Lutheran Publication House.

79

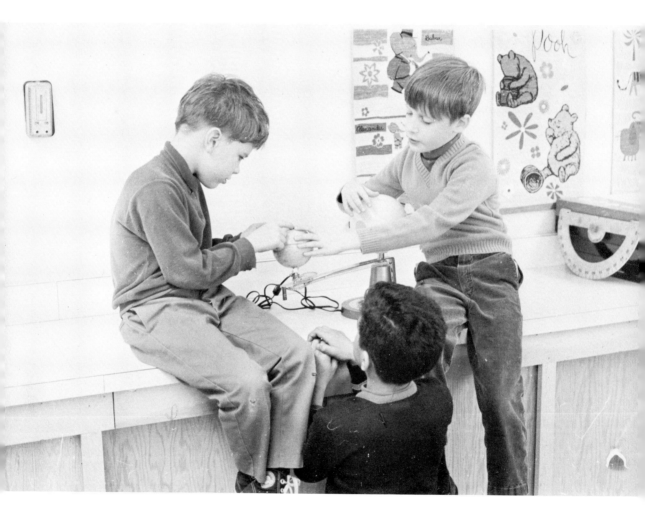

6. Exploring, Experimenting, Investigating

"Beautiful Savior, King of Creation!"

I hear — and I forget
I see — and I remember
I do — and I understand.
— Ancient Chinese Proverb

OBJECTIVES

To help the child —

1. To participate actively in exploring God's creation and investigating his own environment.

2. To know, appreciate, and praise God as the Creator and Ruler of the universe.

3. To learn to recognize and apply some elementary basic concepts in his own investigations.

4. To seek present-day scientific knowledge and some cause-and-effect relationships.

5. To recognize God's hand in the constancy of nature and to become aware of its wonders.

6. To keep an open mind while seeking and investigating factual evidence as it pertains to God's creation.

7. To realize each day anew that science is a gift from God and worthy of our study.

8. To grow always closer to his Creator as he uses current discoveries and basic concepts in a study of God's creation.

SCIENCE IS PART
OF EVERYDAY LIVING

Social living and scientific investigation are closely related, for the one has a direct bearing on the other. The young child who orientates himself into a new world by exploring and finding out is thereby becoming a more social creature.

Science for young children is a natural part of their everyday living. With the new approach to science instruction the small child will find himself in a world of explora-

tion and discovery. Each day should be an adventure for him.

A NEW APPROACH

As soon as a child enters God's created world, he becomes a part of his own environment. One of the first things he does is to observe. Even while very young he looks; he sees. He starts to explore his very limited environment — at first only a crib, a playpen, or a nursery.

This is the starting point for his future learning. It is the beginning of an experiential background that will be the basis for his further study. He will use his past experience plus the findings made available to him plus the process of science at his particular level to discover solutions to his problems and projects.

To build good attitudes and to foster clear scientific thinking it is important that science instruction encouraging children to experiment and ask questions begin in the preschool years.

Since science is a study of God's creation and since one's environment is also a gift of God, a Christian teacher will help the children observe the wonders in God's world. She will help them discover the value and reasons for rain, sunshine, changes, growth processes, and all natural phenomena in the created universe. Science, when linked with God's creation, can be one of the most exciting and challenging subjects in which children can actually participate. Since young children are "scientists" by disposition, they question, they feel, they investigate, they are free from preconceived ideas, they are explorers.

By using the new science materials — through which the children learn to observe, classify, measure, use space, build relationships, and communicate observations — discoveries will early lead the children to realize that scientific knowledge is transitory. What is accepted today may be revised tomorrow in the light of new discoveries and new evidence, but the greatness of God stands even after hills and mountains pass away.

Whereas factual information is still necessary in the process approach, emphasis today is on inquiry and experimentation. New science programs at the preschool level are being developed in which little or no information is given to the children. All activities revolve around the materials on hand and the problems to be solved. These new materials are more helpful than a traditional textbook to establish a climate for investigation. However, needs, interests, and abilities still should be considered when setting up a schedule for science activities in the kindergarten.

THE SCIENCE CORNER

A classroom that will inspire the young children to search for answers through direct experimentation must also provide a stimulating environment. Each room, besides the general materials, should provide a place for the children's collections and personal displays. A practical arrangement is a science corner. In this science corner one will find birds' nests, rocks, shells, seeds, plants, and thousands of interesting things that the children may wish to display and talk about. A bird, a turtle, fish, snails, and other pets are all welcome in a modern kindergarten where children may look, question, and enjoy. The aquarium and the terrarium also give untold opportunities to experiment and observe and perhaps to discover. A large magnifying glass adds to the joy of discovery and to the habit of careful observation.

THE AQUARIUM

A square or oblong aquarium is the best. The aquarium should have clean sand; a few natural objects found in streams; and some aquatic plants as ellgrass, milfoil, pondweed, and certain kinds of algae. The florist or pet shop can supply some cultivated varieties.

The aquarium tank should not be too crowded. One gallon of water will accommodate one one-inch fish, one tadpole, one snail, and several water insects. Very small turtles may be used. Have the children bring the animals if possible. Most pet shops will give directions for the care of pets.

THE TERRARIUM

A waterproof container, an empty aquarium, or a large fishbowl can be used for a terrarium. Seeds and plants placed in a terrarium grow under conditions similar to those in a greenhouse. A plain piece of glass for a cover will hold in the warmth and the moisture.

PLANNING THE CURRICULUM

The teacher will play an important part in directing a science program for preschool children.

She will guide the investigation.
She will investigate with the children.
She will encourage discovery by experimentation.
She will exhibit a real scientific attitude.
She will encourage questions that will suggest problems to be solved.

Many science curriculum programs have been developed or are under preparation supported by grants from the National Science Foundation. Great changes and challenges are forthcoming.

In her planning, the kindergarten teacher will want to check the major elementary science curriculum projects listed in the bibliography. Also of value will be the revised chapter (8) on science in Vol. I of *A Curriculum Guide for Lutheran Elementary Schools,* published by Concordia Publishing House.

POINTING THE CHILDREN TO GOD

A Christian teacher never ceases to make reference to the great wonders in God's beautiful world. She will give the children every possible opportunity to observe rain and sunshine; the growth of human beings, plants, and animals; as well as other examples of God's creation and preservation of the world. She will frequently remind her pupils that God made the world and preserves it. She will not miss an opportunity to bring the child closer to God, the mighty Creator and Preserver of all things. In impressing the children with God's power and goodness, she will try to foster gratitude and praise. This she will do not only in the science instruction, but whenever the opportunity presents itself.

FIELD TRIPS, EXCURSIONS

Excursions or field trips can provide valuable educational experiences if they are properly planned. They should be undertaken only if they contribute to planned goals and lead the children into further exploration and discovery.

An excursion of any kind must be planned. The teacher must be familiar with the place and the mode of travel. The children will be prepared for the experience through conversation and previous experiences.

A note to the parents will supply the needed information and also give the teacher a feeling of security, knowing that the parents trust her to take care of their children. A letter may be sent home with the children. It may be duplicated or written by older children and signed by the kindergarten children if they are able, otherwise by the teacher in their name.

PLACES TO VISIT

A wise teacher will also plan to have her children explore the places of interest in the neighborhood by means of field trips. Almost all kindergartens will be within reach of some of the following sources, which will inspire or motivate children to continue to wonder, to question, and to find out. The teacher will have to make a selection of a few places to which the children may safely go.

1. Airport
2. Barbershop
3. Bottling company
4. Bridges
5. Buildings under construction
6. Cafe
7. Factory
8. Farm
9. Filling station
10. Fire station
11. Florist
12. Fruit market
13. Garage
14. Greenhouse
15. Groceries
16. Hardware store
17. Homes — all kinds
18. Hospital
19. Ice plant
20. Laundry
21. Lumberyard
22. Museums
23. Park
24. Pet store
25. Playgrounds
26. Post office
27. Public library
28. Radio station
29. Railroad station
30. Sawmill
31. Steam shovel
32. Truck farm
33. Woods
34. Zoo

Further questions that lead to worthwhile projects sometimes arise from simple fun-demonstrations as listed below.

1. **Air**

   For demonstrating principles use:

   a. the lungs
   b. balloons
   c. inner tubes
   d. paper bags
   e. soap bubbles
   f. bottles
      1) blow in to cause a whistle
      2) immerse in water to cause bubbles
      3) fill with air to float

   Have the children observe:

   a. people and pets breathing
   b. movements of fish in aquarium as they pass water through their gills
   c. ventilation in the room

2. **Wind** — moving air

   Let the children experiment with:

   a. fans
   b. pinwheels
   c. kites
   d. sailboats

e. soap bubbles

f. windmills

g. wind toys

Have them watch:

a. leaves, smoke, clouds, rain, and snow moving in the air

b. puddles of water disappear on a windy day

c. wind drying doll clothes on a clothesline

3. Water

To show uses of water, have the children:

a. wash doll dishes and clothes

b. siphon water in and out of the aquarium

c. water plants and gardens

Let them:

a. observe small puddles when the temperature is below 32°

b. watch for icicles, dew, frost, rain, hail

c. take note of closed bottles of water in freezing temperature

d. observe melting snow

Other topics of interest may develop from:

1. Magnets   4. Electricity
2. Sound   5. Gravity
3. Storms   6. Sun, moon, stars

PLANT LIFE AND GARDENING

Plant life and gardening offer untold opportunities for experimentation and observation. If space permits, making and caring for an outdoor garden is a satisfying experience. After exercise from digging, sowing, and weeding, the children would gain the added enjoyment of seeing the mystery of the growing process and the even greater satisfaction of picking flowers or vegetables from their own garden.

If outdoor space is limited, gardening experiences can be gotten from indoor planting activities or from trips to a greenhouse or nearby garden.

Some suggested activities:

1. Plant bulbs—tulips, hyacinths, crocuses, daffodils.

2. Plant seeds as directed on packages. Identify the different seeds by putting the empty package on a small stick.

3. Make a glass garden or terrarium.

4. Observe flowers and collect seeds in the fall to plant in the spring.

5. Take walks or excursions to see pretty gardens and fields of grain.

ANIMALS

A study of animals is always fascinating to the small child, and many worthwhile units can be built around animals and their habits.

Suggested activities:

1. Keep an animal pet and care for it.

2. Visit the zoo to see many animals and their ways of living.

3. Watch for birds, their homes, their habits.

4. Observe baby animals and their homes.

5. Observe how the different animals eat and sleep and how they care for their young.

Suggested list of animals that interest small children:

1. Birds
2. Squirrels
3. Hens
4. Dogs
5. Kittens
6. White rats
7. Goldfish
8. Guppy fish
9. Turtles
10. Frogs
11. Cocoons
12. Moths
13. Bees
14. Many of the larger animals, such as horses, bears, elephants, cows, camels.

Some of the smaller animals may be brought to school and kept as pets. This will permit close daily observation, as well as training in the care of pets.

THE SEASONS

Small children very often take the progression of the seasons for granted. A Christian teacher will use the commonplace experiences of heat in summer, cold in winter, and many other natural aspects of the seasons to bring about a greater appreciation of the miraculous and wonderful plan of God in all these natural processes.

Through the study of the seasons, a child should:

1. Become aware of God's orderly plan.

2. Learn to appreciate God's laws that serve all mankind.

3. Trust in His protecting care.

4. Learn to become more conscious of all God's gifts to man.

WEATHER CHART

At any time during the year children will delight in keeping their own weather chart. The children can draw in the pictures to represent the various types of weather with colored chalk or with crayons.

Interest in a weather chart is highest during changeable weather, for the children can use many more symbols to represent various kinds of weather. Use the chart periodically, for interest would lag were it in use all the time. This could be the starter for some intensive discovery about the elements — clouds, storms, tornadoes, etc.

THERMOMETER

Some children may be interested in keeping a record of the temperature changes. A thermometer may be made from heavy

OUR WEATHER CHART

MARCH

Sunshine
Snow
Rain
Cloudy

Sunday	Monday	Tuesday	Wednesday	Thursday	Friday	Saturday
	1	2	3	4	5	6
7	8	9	10	11	12	13
14	15	16	17	18	19	20
21	22	23	24	25	26	27
28	29	30	31			

construction paper on which the degrees can be marked. A red ribbon or a narrow strip of red construction paper may be used to indicate the temperature reading. This can be drawn through slits that are cut parallel to the numbers that indicate the degrees.

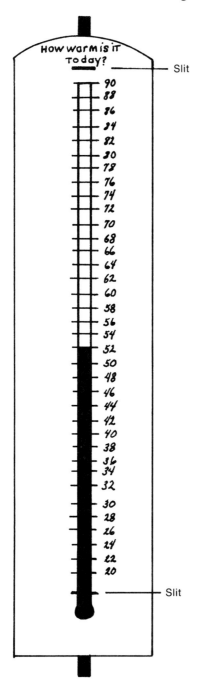

AUTUMN ACTIVITIES

1. Raking leaves
2. Observing leaves change color
3. Watching animals store food away
4. Noticing harvesttime
5. Watching the birds migrate
6. Observing changes in clothing
7. Gathering and preserving pretty leaves

PRESERVING LEAVES

To preserve leaves for a notebook or chart, try covering them with a paste made from borax and water. Let them dry. This will allow the leaves to keep their natural shape. It often preserves the color, too.

To shellac leaves, spread out newspapers to protect tables. Show the children how they may hold a leaf by the stem and paint over it with shellac. This will preserve it for them. Use alcohol to wipe off sticky fingers.

Blueprinting Leaves. Place a pretty leaf on a piece of blueprint paper. Place the leaf and the paper between two pieces of glass. Let the children expose it in the sunlight for about two minutes. Remove the leaf and draw the paper through clear water. Let dry. The imprint of the leaf will fascinate the little observers.

WINTER ACTIVITIES

1. Noticing frost and snow on the ground
2. Observing heavy clothing
3. Seeing heavier fur on animals
4. Playing in the snow
5. Observing winter plants and trees
6. Skating and playing on the ice
7. Feeding winter birds
8. Studying snowflakes under a microscope or magnifying glass
9. Cutting "snowflakes" from folded paper

SPRING ACTIVITIES

1. Noticing the rainfall and storms
2. Observing birds on trees and flowers
3. Watching grass grow
4. Taking walks to notice the return of birds
5. Observing the changes to lighter weight clothing
6. Watering lawns and gardens
7. Picking pussy willows
8. Observing spring flowers
9. Watching birds build their nests
10. Watching baby birds in the nest
11. Observing people planting gardens
12. Watching for the emergence of a moth from a cocoon

Observing Cocoon. Tie the cocoon to a twig and place it in a shoe box with a net over one end or over the top. Moisten the cocoon occasionally with water to keep it soft.

SUMMER ACTIVITIES

Many children go away for the summer months, so it will be wise to prepare the children for a greater appreciation of the wonders of God in different parts of the country. These are common experiences, some of which all may enjoy during the summer season:

1. Swimming and playing on the beach
2. Having picnics in parks and in the woods
3. Taking boat rides
4. Hiking
5. Visiting on farms
6. Observing mountains, rivers, lakes, and perhaps oceans
7. Watching summer storms
8. Flying in airplanes
9. Observing the long summer days
10. Seeing crops and garden vegetables grow

7. Enjoying the Arts

A little child can't read or write
And sometimes cannot talk too well—
But he can show what's in his heart
By free expression through his art.

ART

OBJECTIVES IN ART

1. To develop in the child an appreciation of all beautiful things in God's creation.

2. To stimulate in the child a desire to create beautiful things.

3. To give the child many opportunities to express himself through various art media.

4. To help the child become independent and original in his creative thinking.

5. To help the child experiment, explore, shape, and invent.

6. To help the child discover a few simple principles of art, the fascination of color, and a wise use of materials.

7. To help the child develop desirable work habits and proper attitudes toward his own achievement and that of others.

8. To encourage art as a means of self-expression.

ART IS AN IMPORTANT MEANS OF EXPRESSION

Perhaps one of the most common forms of expression used by small children is art—drawing and painting. They learn quite early to express their ideas by this means. And little boys and girls have ideas! They love to express them, but since they are not yet able to write them down, they express themselves very ably and willingly in the form of art. They can "write down" their thoughts with crayons, paints, and charcoal, and can also give expression to their feelings and ideas with clay, papier-mâché, and other art media.

Let children draw their ideas. Let them scribble their ideas down in any form that appeals to them. Help them, guide them, and encourage them, but don't inhibit them.

Many times the small child's creative expression is only a simple emotional reaction to his everyday activities and can only be interpreted by himself. His picture does not represent so much what he sees as what he feels! This is important in a child's early growth in art. Sometimes it is wise not even to ask him what his picture is. He will be sure to tell you if he wants you to know.

Some children will be full of ideas and ready to express them freely, but sometimes experiences must be provided for the less imaginative so that ideas may come forth from them also. The artwork will then quite naturally grow out of the experiences gained from the various activities. The timid child is sometimes the most creative and the most sensitive to beauty, but needs fuller experiences to get started. He, too, will tell his story through some art media.

SET UP A STIMULATING ENVIRONMENT

A teacher, conscious of the child's natural abilities and of the forces that bring out these abilities, will set up an environment with interesting and appropriate materials and media. Paints, crayons, clay, paste, scissors, charcoal, easels, large paper, and pasteboard will stimulate the desire in the child to use them for self-expression. At first the child will, perhaps, only experiment with the different media—feel them, play with them, or pound them. Later he will, with encouragement and inspiration, use the various media for self-expression, enjoyment, inner satisfaction, and creativity. He will gain confidence in his own ability.

When a teacher sees a child start to work, she may say: "Here's a brave little fellow who gets started right away." Other boys and girls will want the same recognition and will start to take hold and begin to express their thoughts and feelings. Or she may say: "Just make your picture your own way. We will like it."

Free Painting

The beginning kindergarten child will often have no special interest in a perfected skill or in the exact reproduction or the final result, but his interest will be in working with the materials. The activity itself is his chief concern, for through his activity he is showing how he feels.

THE TEACHER'S PART
IN THE ART PROGRAM

The teacher plays a most important part in the art program. Without her the children may never experience those things that are basic to developing wholesome, happy, and creative individuals.

Even though there may be no formal art lesson in the kindergarten, the teacher watches for every chance to encourage, and give inspiration for, better ways of doing without crippling the child's own initiative and cre-

ation. She will guide the children into exploratory and developmental activity. She will proceed on the assumption that every child has creative ability, that he is able to express his ideas in his own way. Through a proper attitude toward his efforts and by help in the techniques to be used, his ability can become more creative in expressing his ideas.

When the children are allowed to work spontaneously and freely, they seek help and advice, which the teacher must give cautiously. She will never do the work for the child, but may give a hint here and a pat on the back there, after which the child will usually continue on his own. A child wants to be reassured that you will like his work. At times the teacher will step out of the picture completely and let the children be on their own, solving their own problems and learning from observation of the other children. When the children go ahead on their own ideas, have differences of opinion, and show some self-assertion in defending them, the teacher will praise rather than criticize them and their sincere efforts. All the while she will observe and see how she may be of help.

STIMULATING THE TIMID CHILD

Stimulating the child who is timid and too cautious to express himself freely is sometimes a difficult task. The teacher will free the child of all fear of defeat, encourage him to play with the media, and slowly capture his interest, perhaps with the subject that fascinates him the most. The subject should be made as interesting as possible, so that the child will want to put it on paper. When once he is full of ideas, his pictures will spill out somewhere. The teacher will try to keep the picture idea coming and developing through praise and encouragement and through keeping the environment congenial. She will be near to encourage the most feeble efforts and to accept sincerely the child's own creation, be it ever so crude and simple. She will respect the product as the work of a child, without imposing adult standards upon it. Nor will she direct the lesson to be done according to a pattern so that all creativity is lost.

KEEPING THE CHILDREN'S POINT OF VIEW

The teacher will learn to view all art from the children's point of view and to appreciate it graciously, for children work best when their work is appreciated. She will avoid negative criticism, which may develop in the child a desire to please the teacher rather than to express himself freely. It is better to treat the child's work casually than critically. The children will soon learn to share their ideas, make certain decisions together, and also respect the ideas and rights of others. They will even begin to evaluate their projects and often look for the suggestions and comments of the teacher.

The teacher will watch for every opportunity to bring into her suggestions some basic principles of art and the functional and proper use of art media. But she will at the same time study the child and the reaction of his mind and body, so she can guide his total growth, remembering that the growing process is more important than the art product—the child more important than the picture.

Drawing and painting will then not be taught as a lesson, but will be used in the kindergarten as a means of telling, of doing, of seeing, of enjoying, and of sharing.

WHAT SHALL THE CHILD DRAW?

Now the question arises: "What shall the child draw?" Since art is an expression from within and since every child feels different inside, one cannot prescribe a course of study for art in the kindergarten. A skillful teacher will encourage expression of ideas that grow out of the day's activities.

Everyday occurrences, such as snowfall, rain, the changing of leaves, play, the coming of winter, winds, flowers and trees, activities in the community, farm life, animals and birds, the zoo, the circus, the church and its activities, in fact, any activity that is carried on in the kindergarten, will suggest abundant creative art activity.

Stories are wonderful avenues for self-expression. Rhymes, poems, songs, records are likely to give rise to ideas for self-expression. Children will be eager to select their own medium and to use it to express their special ideas.

All pictures need not necessarily "tell a story." Some can be just beautiful things or interesting designs. Each child should be encouraged to give his own interpretation, not one that he feels may please the teacher.

RELIGION AND ART

Perhaps the religion lesson will give impetus to a delightful art experience. The stories in the Bible lend themselves most excellently for creative expression. The Flood, David and Goliath, and Joseph's coat are but a few examples of how these stories can stimulate expression. The Feeding of the Five Thousand may introduce a unit on "Food" or on "Gifts from God" and can call forth much creative expression on the part of the children. If the teacher teaches creatively, there will be no dearth of ideas for art expression in religion. The teacher will not ask the children to draw or paint something to look like something else, nor will she ask them to copy a picture in a book or on a wall. A child wants to draw what he feels or sees, be it ever so crude, for his imagination supplies the rest. A young child approaches all experiences creatively when freed to do so.

In a good art program the children will be given the richest experiences possible, will be encouraged to work with a great variety of materials, will be helped to explore many new ways of doing things so that their potentialities may develop to the fullest extent. Though they may never become artists, they can all become lovers of art and use it as a means of self-expression, communication, and enjoyment.

MATERIALS

Besides the child being supplied with experience, he must be supplied with the materials with which to work. Use large pieces of paper for drawing and painting.

creative projects if materials and motivation are in evidence. A large supply of usable materials—clay, finger paint, sponges, screens, cloth, string, colored paper, paste, etc.—ought to be accessible at all times.

DISPLAY OF CHILDREN'S WORK

After children have expressed themselves and their ideas on paper or through

Have large crayons and plenty of vivid powder paints and large brushes on hand. There will be no place in a modern kindergarten for the mere coloring in of patterns drawn or duplicated by the teacher or for filling in of outline pictures as found in coloring books. These trite activities, with an overemphasis on crayons, will give way to more

various other media, the teacher should display the work—not only the best, but at times all the work, the crude as well as the nearly perfect—so that every child's work receives recognition. The room with its decorations should at all times be clean and orderly. It must never give the effect of a showroom with only perfect work displayed—but rather of a room full of ideas and experiences of young children. Little children like to have a part in decorating their room, and they want to feel that they have made the things that are displayed. They like to see drawings hanging around the walls. The room should be a gallery of children's expressions showing their sensitivity to the world about them and the innermost expressions of their personality.

PRINCIPLES TO KEEP IN MIND

A teacher ought to keep the following principles in mind. These principles are not to be taught to the children in so many words, but absorbed by them under the guidance and skill of the teacher.

1. **Encourage Big Drawings.** Large drawings will encourage the children to draw more naturally and gain for themselves more physical satisfaction. They will put less strain on the children's eyes and small muscles and will give them a great deal more satisfactory emotional release. If drawing, painting, and construction are worthwhile activities, then they are worth large pieces of paper. Praise the first signs of large drawings. Tell the children to use all the paper and make large and strong drawings. Ask them to "bump" all the sides of the paper.

2. **Keep the Artwork Moving.** Sometimes children start out with enthusiasm and then lag behind or give up entirely. A sincere compliment starts things going again.

3. **Encourage Interest in Color.** Do not direct which colors are to be used. Let the child experiment with color combinations. He will find out how to obtain the things he wants to show. A few tips here and there are always welcomed.

4. **Draw Attention to Rhythm in Drawing and Painting.** Let the children pull things in the same direction. They will enjoy this. They may call it "swing" and at the same time absorb an important art principle.

5. **Minimize Mistakes.** Often children will say, after a few strokes: "I spoiled mine." Say to them: "We are very unhappy when you spoil something. Don't tell all the children. Keep it a secret and start over." This will discourage a waste of paper and encourage new and greater effort. Use cheap newsprints so that children may "spoil" a few picture ideas.

6. **Keep Your Ideas Out of the Picture as Much as Possible.** Give your ideas only when there is a real dearth of ideas among the children, and then only give a hint and wait for someone to catch the idea and expound it.

7. **How to Display the Work.** It is a good idea at times to pick up a drawing that illustrates an idea in a fantastic or unique way and show it casually to the children. Let the children tack their own drawings up on the bulletin boards. Change the display frequently, so that the children may take their pictures home while the interest is high.

Put the pictures on the children's eye level so they can enjoy them. Exhibit all other craft work or projects, too, so the children can see them and enjoy them together.

ENCOURAGE CREATIVE EXPRESSION

A teacher interested in the growth of art in small children will do everything possible to encourage the creative expression in the little child. She will weave in a few basic principles of mechanics and will help the child correlate eye, hand, brain, and imagination. She will help him develop a preference for beauty and color, heighten and make more alert his sense perceptions, and express his inner feelings in a form that is satisfying to him. In this way she will be helping him become an art-loving child, a respecter of God's beautiful creations, and an "artist" in his own right.

MUSIC

OBJECTIVES IN MUSIC

1. To encourage the child to praise and thank God with his voice.

2. To help the child sing naturally and spontaneously.

3. To develop a love for singing in groups and alone.

4. To make singing so attractive that each child will want to participate.

5. To provide an opportunity for self-expression.

6. To teach the child a few easy little songs by rote that he can sing at home as well as in school.

7. To set up occasions for listening to good music.

8. To help the nonsinging or uncertain singers to succeed in one way or another. Help them find their singing voice.

9. To provide opportunity for all to participate in musical activities of all kinds.

10. To watch for and help develop special talents in music.

THE IMPORTANCE OF MUSIC

Music is invaluable in building an integrated Christian personality and a happy life, for it allows freedom of response according to the individual's needs and his background of experience. Music, a vital part of the child's living, should be a spontaneous activity in the kindergarten program, being heard many times during the day. It may break forth during a cleanup period, a religion lesson, or even on a walk through the park. It cannot be pigeonholed into 10 or 15 minutes during the day. The teacher will carefully observe to see where she can enter in naturally with her songs and rhythms during the day. In this way music will function at all times with the emphasis on the happiness and relaxation it brings to the child.

Even the very young child responds to music. He moves his body to rhythm, and he delights in making up his own songs. Let the kindergarten child continue with these activities.

SINGING

Singing, rhythms, listening, and creating are all important in the kindergarten program, but perhaps the most universal and most popular approach to music for the young child is through singing.

No one list of songs for the kindergarten can be drawn up and used as a basic list, because the songs will quite naturally grow out of the various activities. However, when selecting songs for the units and activities, it is wise to ask the following questions:

1. Is the subject matter and content within the scope and interest of the small child?

2. Is the song short, and the melody easy and singable?

3. Is there enough repetition for the child to learn quickly and to enjoy?

4. Is the range between middle D and an octave above it, or thereabouts?

5. Does the song have a marked rhythm and the same tempo throughout?

6. Does the subject matter make sense to the children?

LEARNING TO SING IN TUNE

Since music is mostly for the small child's enjoyment, very little emphasis should be placed on the actual techniques of singing other than stressing the desire to sing in tune with a free, natural tone. Some of the children, if systematically guided, will soon learn to match tones and in time will feel a definite responsibility for helping the nonsingers match the tones. After the children can match tones, they will learn to sing. From then on it means building for themselves new melody patterns for their new songs. This takes time and patience and a great deal of repetition, so that the patterns become memorized and soon transferred to other songs.

The best helping instrument is the teacher's own voice, and next are the voices of the "in-tune" singers—those who can already carry a melody independently of the teacher or an instrument. The teacher will group her children so that the "out-of-tune" singers and those who have difficulty in matching tones will be near her, on a rug, in a circle, or on some small chairs, with the "in-tune" singers right behind them. In this way they will receive help from the teacher and the children who already have good pitch control.

Many kindergarten children never learn to sing, because their teachers fail to teach them how to "listen" to the tones they are to make. Too often they are allowed day after day to sing in conversational tones, building in their own minds the mistaken notion that they are really singing.

TEACHING A SONG

After the teacher has presented the song clearly and accurately to the group, she will constantly remind the children to sing lightly, softly, and sweetly, so that they will become conscious of pretty tones and will want to reproduce them.

It will not be necessary to make an elaborate introduction before teaching a new song to the group. When the occasion arises, it is wise to start singing. Say little about the song, then sing it for the children. They will soon join in on a refrain or on a line or two. Perhaps they will start singing at the last line, but that is acceptable. As a rule teach the song in its entirety, not in parts. The learning of the song will be gradual, but repeated efforts will soon bring results.

Children must be commended for every effort and never laughed at by the teacher or by the group. This would take away the plea-sure and joy from singing. Children should also be encouraged, but never forced, to sing alone.

If the teacher cannot sing, she will have to rely on the piano or some other instrument for correct pitch and melody and use recordings. A record player is a must in a kindergarten room. Individual earphones, which children can use at their leisure, encourage good listening habits.

SIMPLE PRINCIPLES

1. Know your song thoroughly before attempting to teach it to your children, and, if possible, present the song without referring to a book.

2. Show enthusiasm in the song you choose.

3. Repeat the song often, day after day.

4. Choose only a few songs and teach them well.

5. Encourage the faintest effort.

6. Never allow the group to show disfavor to those with a great degree of atonality.

7. Enjoy the song with your children.

PRESENT THE SONG
AS THE CHILDREN ARE TO SING IT

In presenting songs to children, the teacher, to the best of her ability, renders every selection in a musical and artistic way. She tries to use a light, easily produced tone true to pitch and of pleasant quality. She pronounces the words distinctly and accurately. In brief, she attempts to render the song as she wishes the children to sing it.

Generally a song is taught to the children in its entirety. However, sometimes it seems advisable, because of vocal difficulties, to treat a single phrase as a separate unit. Immediately following, the phrase is connected with the other phrases, and the entire song is sung again. But let it be an appreciation more than a skill to be taught.

In planning her musical program for the

kindergarten, a teacher sometimes wonders, perhaps with a degree of trepidation, whether she has enough musical background to teach the children properly. She need not be a trained musician to be successful in the musical program with the children and to direct the day's musical activities. She must, however, have a love for music and a keen understanding of how the young child learns, together with a knowledge of what part music plays in the life of the small child.

VARIOUS KINDS OF SINGERS

Before entering on the discussion of the different musical activities, it might be well to recognize the various kinds of singers that will be found in any normal group. This will aid the teacher in placing proper emphasis on the helping technique needed for each individual child. One usually thinks of four different kinds of singers.

1. **The Independent Singers** — Those who can, without the aid of an instrument or another voice, sing on correct pitch, or those who can carry a melody alone.
2. **The Dependent Singers** — Those who can carry a melody with the aid of the independent singers, the teacher, or an instrument, but not alone.
3. **Uncertain Singers** — Those who have difficulty with a whole song but are able to match tones. They are often the fearful ones and are afraid to try. However, they learn rapidly.
4. **The Out-of-Tune Singers** — Those who cannot match tones at all or are completely untrue to pitch. Most of these succeed after patient assistance.

As has been suggested, it is sometimes advisable to arrange the children in such a way that the less able are placed next to better singers who will play the role of "helpers." These helpers, who are independent singers, will be a great aid to the teacher when working on new melodies.

Another way in which to help the uncertain or out-of-tune singers is to seat them with the better or more sure singers in the back, so that the children in the front hear correct tones: Thus:

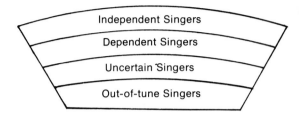

THE ENVIRONMENT IS IMPORTANT

The child's world is filled with music. The TV, radio, and record player constantly bring music into the home. So a kindergarten teacher will want to set up an environment that will foster rich and rewarding musical experiences for her children.

Musical experiences will go on all day, for music is a part of the children's living and is just as necessary in the life of a child as flowers, pretty pictures, and storybooks.

Since music is an expression of emotional well-being, of contentment, of pleasure, and of relaxation, it should be considered as a natural thing in which everyone may take part, and not as an experience set aside for only a few gifted people. So after the environment is set up, a teacher will see to it that everyone participates freely, even if his "booming one-tone" may spoil the effect at first. She can work on tone after all feel that they belong and are accepted. It is wise in the beginning to sing freely and with not too much teaching technique in mind.

Most spontaneous singing will develop naturally during the day, as will other activities, such as rhythmic experiences, listening, and experimenting. It will grow out of the play life of the children. This type of music is part of the children. This type of music is part of social development. It indicates well-being and a feeling of security.

As members of a group, children must also have a feeling of working together and respecting the rights of others, so a teacher will also have a planned but flexible singing time. It should be an informal gathering in which she teaches some of the fundamental principles of singing in a relaxed learning atmosphere.

SING FOR PLEASURE

If a teacher thoroughly enjoys singing, she can do much to stimulate her pupils to sing when suitable occasions arise. A song repertoire can be built up by frequently singing the old songs, perhaps starting with the familiar nursery rhymes, and then going on to new ones. A teacher will have a variety of charming little songs, exercises, and finger plays that she can sing spontaneously when beginning her "singing time."

When teaching small children to sing, select songs in the proper range, but do not force the child to stay in this range when he is learning. Rather, as in other fields, begin where the child is and adapt the pitch of the songs to meet his range. If a child learns to sing in tune in his natural range, an understanding teacher can easily help him develop a wider and more uniform range. It is easier for a teacher to adjust to the child's voice than for the child to change his range. This is wise when first beginning so that the child experiences some degree of success.

With continued and patient help most little children will learn to sing by listening and singing along, sometimes perhaps only humming. In a few cases it may become necessary to work more consistently with a child's voice. If this becomes necessary, it is wise to do a little extra singing privately so that the child gains confidence in his own performance before he is asked to sing before the group. Soon he will be happy to perform.

POINTS TO REMEMBER

Remember that children have small, delicate vocal organs; therefore:

1. Encourage them always to sing lightly and true to pitch.
2. Pick songs with simple, clean-cut melody throughout.
3. Repeat the songs often.
4. Praise every effort in which a child participates.
5. Do not force participation. Encourage it.
6. Use your songs throughout the day, and especially use your religious songs, for music makes an immeasurable contribution to the spiritual life of children. What, for example, can be more appropriate than a song about Jesus during a storm!

Children will be delighted to express their feelings in song if they are encouraged and helped over difficulties until they gain more and more confidence and power of expression.

RHYTHM

Music experiences are an integral part of children's school experience. They sing when happy, when sad, when disappointed. Rhythm is seen in everything little children do. They skip, run, jump, clap their hands, and show enthusiasm in bodily movements of all kinds. They sweep the floor, go up and down a teeter-totter, and bounce balls. Rhythm prevails everywhere, from the heartbeat of a little child to the most intricate movements of an artist.

A teacher of little children will base her rhythms on the children's crude motor activities in play, their natural abilities and interests, and their moods and temperaments. They will soon pick up the idea of rhythm and create some of their own verses or phrases. The music of simple folk tunes and of games and songs makes excellent accompaniment for running, skipping, galloping, or other movements. Have the children listen and do as the music "says."

Some of the natural rhythms are:

1. Walking
2. Running
3. Tiptoeing
4. Sliding
5. Bending
6. Skipping
7. Swinging
8. Swaying
9. Turning
10. Stretching
11. Clapping and tapping
12. Galloping
13. Hopping

Rhythms are fundamental in:

1. Building and disciplining the body.
2. Developing creativity.
3. Developing coordination.
4. Helping children grow in social living—working cooperatively.
5. Stimulating the imagination.

Large bells, hoops, scarfs, ropes, and various rhythm instruments are essential helps in the rhythm program of the kindergarten.

Most rhythms can be taught as part of the daily activities. The unconscious rhythmic quality in many of the ordinary movements of the children as they move around and play in the room are good starting points.

It is fun to start the children off in creating their own rhythms during their activities; for example, as they hop, say, "Here I go, hop, hop, hop. I go and never stop, stop, stop."

It must be understood that a child's progress will be dependent on his muscular coordination, his self-confidence, and his ability to express his feelings with bodily movements.

Do not confuse the child with too many techniques. Let him master one at a time as he begins to feel and see his own progress.

LISTENING

Children grow best when they are given a variety of musical experiences. Some may experience difficulty in finding their singing voices or in matching tones, so that they are reluctant when it comes to actual participation in these particular musical experiences. However, they find satisfaction and pleasure in other musical activities. They like to listen—to hear music and thereby develop favorable attitudes and growing interest. The kindergarten teacher will also provide a good listening program for her pupils.

She will, first of all, provide a good piano that will be kept in perfect pitch and perhaps painted to harmonize with the rest of the room.

Many opportunities must be afforded the small child to hear differences—starting perhaps with the difference in noise between a tap on the table and a tap on a xylophone or the difference between one piano key and another. From these very simple beginnings an appreciation program can be developed, and the children can be trained to listen purposefully, even if the purpose at first is sheer enjoyment. Small children cannot be expected to "listen quietly" unless helped by the teacher through many suggestions and hints as to how they can discover fine experiences in music.

The teacher may ask the little ones to respond to the music by physical movements or perhaps to listen for a familiar rhythmic movement. They may interpret the music with free expression, acting it out or drawing pictures to match what it says.

A good listening program will provide constant opportunity for various kinds of creative expression—drums, stretched strings, homemade and school-made xylophones and marimbas, bells, water glasses, flutes, combs, and others. The teacher will capture every occasion—the first snow, a game, a poem—during the day to foster creative interpretation and free and wholehearted participation of the children.

MUSIC APPRECIATION MUST BE CAUGHT

Music cannot be taught, at least not the real appreciation of it. It must be caught and must become an integrated part of the child's living. It can be used for enjoyment, for learning, for interpretation and dramatization, and for a quiet rest period.

CRAFTS

OBJECTIVES IN THE CRAFTS

1. To develop a liking for using the hands in making things for self and others.

2. To help the child plan and create things he would like to make.

3. To develop the coordinative skills required in working with the hands.

4. To encourage the child to use crafts as a worthwhile hobby.

5. To help the child grow in the art of working together with others and of sharing materials.

6. To give the child a feeling of accomplishment and joy in making something for others.

CHILDREN LIKE TO MAKE THINGS

All little boys and girls like to make things. They delight in making things all by themselves and at times carrying them home to Father or Mother, using them for a party, or giving them to unfortunate children elsewhere. They thrill to the creation they have made.

DISTINCTION BETWEEN ARTS AND CRAFTS

The craft program must not be confused with art education. A teacher must never feel that she has completed her assignment of teaching art when her children have made little favors or gifts for others. She must be aware of the fact that it is her duty to help the child create, to draw and paint freely, to design, and to express feeling in all sorts of ways through all kinds of media. Making something from a pattern or after a form made by the teacher is not art, but it should find a place under the name of crafts.

WHEN TO USE CRAFTS

Occasion arises during the year, at special holidays, festivals, and birthdays, when the teacher may want the children to make some little gift or remembrance. She will show the children how to proceed but will be careful not to have them follow a stereotyped way of doing. She will leave enough room for creative ability and accept any ideas from the children. Even in the crafts children can learn to be creative, and a good teacher will accept this way of expression.

DO NOT EXPECT TOO MUCH

Little children will not do things as well as their big brothers and sisters, but it is far better to have work not quite so well done than to have the older children or the teacher cut out and paste up the work for the small children.

When working on a craft program, select things to make that can easily be made by kindergarten children, and then do not expect a finished product. Discuss the ideas given by the children, supply the media, show how, if necessary, and let the children go to work. Avoid patterns and outlined drawings to fill in. They pass time, but they do not have educational value, foster creative thinking, or arouse creative action.

The following suggestions are to help guide the teacher in selecting some things that children enjoy doing.

CRAYON WORK

Crayons, which are probably used more extensively than any other medium in the kindergarten, should be large and flat if possible. It is good to have an eight-color set for each pupil, or each table may be supplied with sets of different colors that the children may use cooperatively.

It is not necessary to tell a child just how he should use his colors. He will find a way that is pleasing and satisfying to him, one that will express his ideas. Some children prefer

Paper Plate Designs

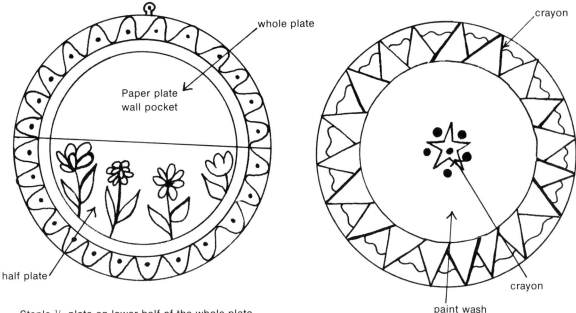

Staple ½ plate on lower half of the whole plate

to press hard, others will use the crayons very lightly. There is no right or wrong way of using them, so let the child feel free to color as he wishes. If a child learns to hold his crayon as he does a piece of chalk, he will be able to work more freely.

If suggestions are to be made that may improve the technique, they can be made by praising the child who has succeeded, and others will soon take the hint.

After the crayons are broken, it is a good idea to have a large box into which all crayons may be pooled. This is for general use. Flat and peeled-off crayons come in handy for filling in sky and water or grass. When used flat-side, they are the best crayons with which to fill in large areas on paper or on a wall frieze.

With crayons children can draw almost anything: trees, houses, animals, birds, flowers, toys, buildings, fruits and vegetables, people. They can illustrate stories, draw experiences and trips, make cards for the

sick and color all their craft projects. They can also color on cloth, paper plates, paper bags, and the like.

After children have used crayons, they often enjoy painting a light paint-wash over the colored surface and watch how the paint runs off the colored surface but remains on the uncolored. Paper plates lend themselves very effectively to this type of coloring and painting.

Have the children color a simple design around the plate and in the center. They will then apply the wash with a brush. The wash should be very light. Let the child experiment with the paint until he has the wash he wants to use.

After the plate is dry, shellac it to make it permanent.

When using crayons on cloth, select cheap, unbleached muslin, cut it in pieces, and have the children color some simple design on it. Stretch the material and fasten with thumbtacks on beaverboard or other firm board, or

CRAYON ON CLOTH

Table Mat or Scarf

Fringe the edges, and have the children color the design on the cloth

Book Cover

Cloth on which crayon has been applied is pasted on construction paper to decorate a book cover

Simple designs can be put on doll dresses made from inexpensive materials or used for Indian outfits made from flour sacks

A Simple Puppet

Dresses

A Bag Decorated for Valentines

A Mask

place securely in an embroidery hoop. A stencil may first be made and placed over the muslin and colored over, if desired. To set the color, place the drawing face down on a damp cloth and iron on the reverse side.

PAINT

Powder paint is perhaps next in usefulness in the primary school or kindergarten. The powder paint can be mixed with water to get the desired shade and consistency. The children will enjoy mixing their own paints, especially if they are given the opportunity to use only the three primary colors, red, yellow, blue, and to mix them to get orange, green, and violet.

To save expense these powder paints can be mixed with calcimine. A good brand of school paint is strong enough to mix with at least two parts of cheaper paint or calcimine. There are many kinds of paints and paint materials on the market today.

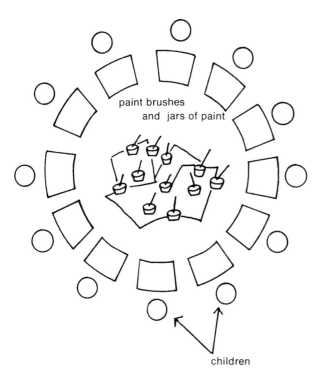

paint brushes
and jars of paint

children

Position on floor

Children like to paint on the floor. Place small containers on the floor in the center of a circle, and let the children sit on the floor around the paint with a large piece of newsprint or newspaper in front of them. In this way they can get the paint they need and can at the same time see what others are doing. They love to see each other's paintings and handcraft projects. Let the children paint freely. Let them experiment. Each stroke of the brush will mean something to them, and they will gladly interpret it for you.

Powder paint washes off clothes quite easily, but a very practical apron may be made from a man's old shirt or from plastic material.

FINGER PAINTING

Children like to finger-paint. They enjoy the thrilling adventure and the creative experience.

Finger paint and finger-paint paper are rather expensive. Undue expense may be saved by using any gloss-finish paper, such as butcher paper or smooth wrapping paper. Finger paint can be made according to the following recipes:

A

1. Use ordinary white calcimine.

2. Mix with water until creamy.

3. Add a bit of glycerine to the mixture. (This slows up the drying process.)

4. Add colored powder paint to the mixture.

B

½ cup dry starch.
1 ⅓ cups boiling water.
½ cup soap flakes.
1 teaspoon glycerine.
Water colors or vegetable coloring.

1. Mix starch with a little cold water to make paste.

2. Add boiling water and boil till clear and glossy.

3. Add soap flakes and stir in well.

4. Add glycerine.

5. Pour into jars and add coloring.

6. Allow to cool before using.

C

1. Measure into large pan 6 cups of cold water.

2. Blend in gradually:
   1½ cups wheat paste
   ½ cup soap flakes

3. For preservative and fragrance add cologne, oil of wintergreen, or cloves.

4. Divide mixture in half if two colors are desired.

5. Blend in 6 tablespoons of powder paint to equal mixture. Leave ½ uncolored if desired. After colorless finger paint is on paper, child shakes on powder paint of his choice.

D

Two or three tablespoons of liquid starch may be poured on the wet paper, one-half teaspoon powdered paint added and mixed as the child paints with it.

Moisten the smooth paper on both sides in a sink if possible, otherwise in a large, flat pan or with a sprinkling can. Smooth it out on a flat surface, a table or the floor, over which newspapers have been spread. Give each child some paint and encourage him to use his hands freely, his whole hand, his arm, and perhaps his elbow.

For sheer enjoyment the children may paint on oilcloth, from which their paintings can be washed off many times. With small children this activity and the freedom to create is more important than the finished product. Encourage this freedom by sometime painting to music.

PAINTING WITH THINGS

Children will enjoy bringing all sorts of things—sticks, screws, nails, etc.—to school and using them to make designs. Paints will be mixed to a creamy consistency, and the children will dip their objects into the paint, using them to make various designs on paper or cloth.

Ask the children to use only one or two items in one design and repeat.

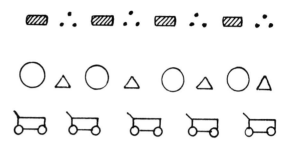

In fact almost anything the child brings can be used for a print design. Some children can handle a carrot or a potato for simple block printing.

STRING DESIGN

Let the children dip a piece of string into paint. Then let them lay it all twisted up on one side of a folded piece of paper 12 by 18 inches. Fold over the paper, and press down. Then let the child pull out the string. The design is imprinted on both sides of the paper.

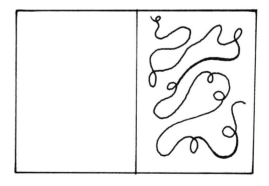

PAPER CUTTING

Little children can spend many happy hours cutting out things. They can cut things out of magazines, catalogs, and newspapers for their charts and booklets. A group frieze or collage is fun to make with magazine pictures. At first the edges will be quite jagged, but the teacher must not expect more from little fingers that are just learning to use small muscles.

Children can also learn to cut freehand and will delight in cutting flowers, trees, crosses, and animals for the windows and bulletin boards. Give the children cheap paper so that they can experiment over and over again. Occasionally have them tear paper into simple shapes or into small pieces to be used for mosaics.

CLAY

If you want your children to enjoy playing with clay, use the regular oil-base clay that comes in various colors and can be used over and over again. It is clean and inexpensive. They will even enjoy softening it with their warm hands. If, however, you wish to have the children make something more permanent and perhaps a little more creative, try using real clay. This can be bought in powder form and mixed or in package or boxed form. It can also be dug from the earth.

You may wish to experiment with some of the following recipes for modeling material:

A

1. Mix:
   1 1/3 cup sifted flour
   1 2/3 cup non-iodized salt
   1 1/4 tablespoon alum powder

2. Add 3/4 cup water and stir.
   For solid color add food coloring to water. For marbelized effect add pigment to dry batch. If wrapped in damp cloth and piece of plastic, material can be reused. When dry, forms can be painted.

B

1. Add 2 cups salt to 2/3 cup water heated.

2. Add 1 cup cornstarch to 1/2 cup cold water.

3. Combine salt and cornstarch mixtures and stir quickly.
   Keeps indefinitely in plastic wrap.

C

1. Mix:
   1 cup salt
   2 cups flour

2. Gradually add about 1/4 – 1/2 cup water and 2 teaspoons cooking oil and stir.

There is no special technique in modeling; your best tools are your fingers. However, certain working rules should be followed, but the teacher should interfere as little as possible in the child's creative project.

Keep the clay soft enough to squeeze, and let the children play with it and squeeze it before attempting to make anything. The children may at first just be content to make a ball or a very simple ashtray or candle holder. If you should wish to join parts together, use "Slip." This is a thin mixture of clay and water, which you can slip in between the places to be joined.

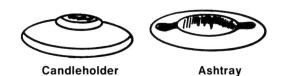

Candleholder   **Ashtray**

Press candle in clay to make the hole. Then remove it while the clay dries

Keep clay in a crock and cover with a wet cloth to keep from getting hard.

If you wish to have your things harden without firing, mix some dextrin with the clay (one part dextrin to five parts of powdered clay.)

You may wish to make an imprint of the child's hand in clay.

Some necessary equipment for clay work would include: newspapers, masonite or wooden boards covered with plastic, a worktable, and shellac to coat the finished product.

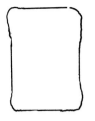

Flatten the Clay

Have child press his hand on it

PUPPETS

Puppets on Clothespins

Puppets Made from Paper Bags

The children stick their hands in the sacks and make the puppets act and talk

RHYTHM INSTRUMENTS

Children enjoy making their own instruments to use in the many activities involving rhythms. With some help from the teacher, they can make quite a few with a degree of success.

They can bring most of the materials from home and thus feel that they have played an important part in making them.

Simple Tambourine

Let the children color with crayons or paint the outer sides of two paper plates with a fancy design. Put some rice kernels in between the two plates and staple together. Shake to the music.

Jingle Clogs

Cut small pieces of wood, approximately one half by six inches or thereabouts. Sandpaper them until smooth. Have the children collect soda-pop bottle tops. Make nail holes through the center of the tops. Nail three or four on the edge of the piece of wood at evenly spaced intervals. If the nails used are smaller than the nail holes, the bottle tops will jingle quite readily. Shake for rhythm of horses trotting or other rhythms.

Triangles

Old horseshoes will make good triangles. Use old nails or spikes to play with.

Bells

An old pan or face brush from which the bristles have been removed makes an excellent base on which to fasten bells that can be bought in the dime store.

Bells can also be sewed on an elastic band, which can be worn around the hand.

Shakers

Any small cans—fruit juice, baby food—can be painted and filled with rice or beans. Attach a handle through the can. These produce good rattling noises.

Drums

Oatmeal or Pablum boxes are good for drums. They may be painted or covered with wallpaper. If you wish, you may cover the top and bottom with inner tubing and lace together with shoestrings.

The creative teacher will find innumerable ways to have the children work with craft media. The children will love to become involved and by working with the various materials will develop a sense of feeling and perception. As they gain skills in using the materials, they will build a self-concept of worth as "craft artists."

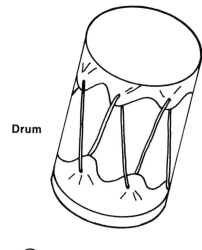

Drum

Simple Tambourine

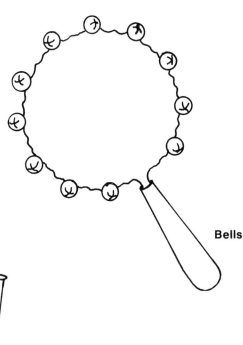

Bells

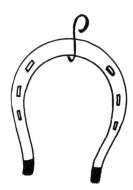

Triangles

Shakers

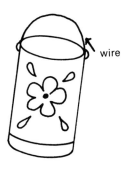

wire

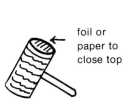

foil or
paper to
close top

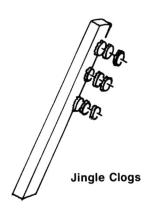

Jingle Clogs

8. The Language Arts

LANGUAGE DEVELOPMENT IN THE KINDERGARTEN

Language arts embraces the many language skills fused into one broad field. In the kindergarten these skills are not separated into distinct categories but grow and develop within the total learning program. They permeate all the subject areas.

These skills develop in the child in relation to his experiential background and his potential for learning. The teacher must evaluate each child's present developmental and achievement level so she may establish a basis for the "pacing" rate of each child.

Since language is a primary ingredient in forming concepts, in solving problems, and in relating to the environment, the teacher will regard it as an instrument of communication, thinking, and feeling.

The two broad areas with which she will be concerned are the *expressive* skills (speaking and writing) and the *receptive* skills (listening and reading). The kindergarten environment will abound in opportunities to speak and to listen. The ability to understand and to use oral communication will be basic to most of the learning experiences.

General Objectives

Objectives for language teaching in the kindergarten should be focused on:

1. Improving the ability to use the communication skills in various ways.

2. Involving the children in activities that foster language growth —

planning	sharing	reporting
speaking	telling	describing
looking	discussing	evaluating

3. Helping children speak in sentences freely and fluently.

4. Developing oral language skills through —

conversation	TV
records	movies
tapes	dramatic plays

5. Enunciating clearly and pronouncing correctly.

6. Developing listening skills through media suggested for oral language skills.

7. Developing writing skills through self-expression recorded by the teacher.

This is an area in which each child will grow at his own rate. On the pages that follow it is not the author's intention to set up a course to follow, but to make suggestions how some of these broader objectives may find expression.

A child needs in his language program—

The sunshine of stimulation
The shade of relaxation
The fertilizer of rich experiences.
—J. Hymes

ORAL EXPRESSION

CHILDREN VARY IN LANGUAGE ABILITY

Children who come to kindergarten vary greatly in their ability to use language. Some can hardly express themselves clearly while others have thousands of words at their command; but all use language to interpret the world about them and through language learn to react to many different situations. Children also love to experiment with different words and phrases, and they love to learn new expressions and use them in their daily conversations. Therefore children should be encouraged to talk, for if they are not permitted to talk, they can never learn to talk well. Talking is basic to language development.

"TALKING TIME"

The conversation hour or "Talking Time" can be one of the brightest spots in the day. Young boys and girls can become quite absorbed in telling or reporting. When they find that people listen to them, they begin to feel secure and accepted in their new surroundings. Children are happy when they are able to say what they mean and to be understood by others.

Group experiences such as walks, trips, stories, records, or filmstrips furnish excellent materials for daily conversation. Through this free-talking time children gain a command of the language, and at the same time they build new concepts and acquire good habits of expression.

A teacher should not be satisfied with idle prattle but should guide the children and help them learn to express themselves well. They should learn when to speak as well as how to speak.

Children will have to be reminded to take turns, to keep to the subject, and to listen when others speak. Corrections by the teacher should be made as unobtrusively as possible, so that the children will not be hampered in the thoughts they wish to express. A suggestion by the teacher or the mere repetition of the correct form will usually bring about the desired results. It is wise to substitute the correct form and let the child go right on talking. He will learn by hearing. It will not be necessary for him to use or repeat the correct form at that time. He will soon use it of his own accord, perhaps the very next time he speaks.

SOME POINTS TO REMEMBER

1. Even a small child, when speaking to a group, should make himself heard.

2. Help the child decide whether or not he has something interesting to talk about. He will soon learn to judge for himself.

3. Has he perhaps told his story before? If so, he should not repeat it unless the others want to hear it again.

4. When a child speaks, have him face the group and look at those to whom he wishes to speak.

5. Encourage the child to use language that

he understands and that will help him tell the story.

6. Help the child develop his creative instinct and increase his powers of imagination.

7. Help the child avoid the use of slang expressions or baby talk.

8. Help the child observe the common courtesies — to listen when others have something to offer, to refrain from undue interrupting, to speak one at a time, not to monopolize.

Oral language is so closely interwoven with the daily life of children that an alert teacher will have to use every possible situation to bring about a wholesome language development. A stimulating school environment will guide the children into fascinating realms and stimulate their imagination, their creativity, their sense of humor, their interest in others, and their desire for information. This in turn will lead them into delightful oral expression.

WRITTEN EXPRESSION

WRITTEN LANGUAGE GROWS OUT OF NEEDS

Written language grows out of real needs of the children, and the teacher should be on the alert to recognize such needs. By doing so she will create an interest and a desire to grow in written expression.

Written language in the kindergarten usually takes the form of dictations by the children. These are recorded on the board or on chart paper by the teacher. The experience charts or chart stories lay the foundation for the original stories the children will write later in the grades. This same procedure is followed when sending notes home, making birthday greetings, etc.

These little notes, composed by the children and printed or duplicated by the teacher, help the children realize that writing is a means of communication and that it is used in their own lives in everyday occurrences. It becomes a functional activity.

OCCASIONS FOR WRITTEN LANGUAGE

If a mother has given a party, the children may send a note like this:

Thank you for the good party. We had fun.

From the Kindergarten

They may invite their mothers to a party in this way:

Mother, come to our 🌲 party at 2 o'clock Dickie 🌲

Or tell things in this way:

News of the day

Jackie has a birthday.

There is a bicycle assembly today at 10:00 o'clock.

Or they may wish to carry home information on their own little notes, like this:

May I go to the airport on Thursday? Sign here. _____

News !
Mom — No school tomorrow.
Teachers meeting.

A picture of me costs 25¢

Pictures that children have made may be labeled like this:

See the turtle. Billy painted it.

Tom made this boat.

The lockers and the children's personal property may be labeled to help them recognize the names of their classmates. In the beginning of the school year it may be advisable to use a picture or a sticker of some kind beside the name so that, if the child should fail to identify his name by the symbols, he may use the picture clue. Thus:

There is little need to label the well-known objects in the room such as piano, desk, chair, vase, or easel, as these things are all known to the children, and the words in isolation would not have much meaning for them. If a teacher wishes to introduce these concepts to the children, it would be better to use the word in a sentence like this:

Listen to the story.
Use the earphones.

Play with the magnets.
You may experiment.

Interesting captions under pictures always appeal to children. All signs and labels should be written in manuscript letters, as these are the forms that the children will use when they start to read and write in a more formal situation.

PREHANDWRITING ACTIVITIES

Writing is not an end in itself, but a tool to express an idea—a means to an end.

The young child usually writes in some way before he enters school. His scribbling is his communication. In time the child realizes that his notes can be sent and received.

Soon he and his age-mates take an active part in dictating the messages. All this helps the child see the need for writing. He is beginning to think of writing as "talk written down."

A kindergarten child has a deep interest in writing his own name. This is his identity. During the year more mature children will ask the teacher how to make letters and words express something they want to tell. When this teaching moment occurs, the teacher should help by showing the correct form. However, children who are neither interested nor ready should not be forced to do something they cannot do.

Anything more formal than this is usually not undertaken in the kindergarten. But all exercises and games involving arm, hand, or finger movement; eye-hand coordination; and muscular control will lay the foundation for the use of the finer muscle development needed in writing.

THE BULLETIN BOARD

The bulletin board is a good medium to develop an interest in the written word and its meaning. Lost-and-found notices may appear from time to time.

Who lost a ?

Items of interest to the children will encourage the children to look at the "News of the Day." Examples:

Count Down!

Did you watch

it on T V?

WEATHER CHART

A "Weather Chart" on which the children record the temperature and the kind of weather develops observation and interest.

Aa - Bb - Cc - Dd - Ee - Ff -
Gg - Hh - Ii - Jj - Kk - Ll - Mm -
Nn - Oo - Pp - Qq - Rr - Ss - Tt -
Uu - Vv - Ww - Xx - Yy - Zz -

Manuscript letter-forms are usually used for beginning writing activities. However, some teachers of young children prefer all capital letters because they are one size.

THE CHILDREN'S OWN STORIES

The dictated story or experience story in which the children give their ideas and the teacher writes out the story in large manuscript letters on oak tag or large construction paper (18 by 36 inches) is a most valuable means for introducing the children to reading as a means of expression. The children can be encouraged to create stories on their own, which need not be perfect — no more than their clay modeling is sculpture nor their dramatic play drama. Their stories are merely a form of creative expression that helps them feel and share their experiences.

After the story has been written on large paper — in manuscript form — by the teacher, the children may draw or paint pictures to match it, and then all together can enjoy "reading" the story as a whole. The story is for them to enjoy and to help them gain the idea of the use of symbols as a medium for recording stories and events. Any group experience lends itself readily for a chart story.

Little stories about the children themselves also make good writing material. These stories make an effective appeal to the children and can easily be put into book form and looked at over and over again.

Look at our guppies,
Mark gave them to us.
Can you count them?
The big one is the
mother.

Stories can be made about their mothers and fathers or sisters and brothers or about any experiences they have had during the day, over the weekend, or on vacations.

Felt pens of different colors are useful when making story charts. Some teachers delight in typing the stories on a primer typewriter and duplicating them for the children.

Our Space Ship

Did you see us in our space ship?

Bobby was the pilot.

Sam was The flight engineer.
Did we go!!
Up and up!

Airplane

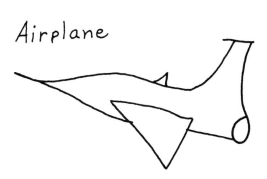

This is a big jet.
It is flying high.
It is flying fast.
It looks like
a big bird
It is flying across
The Atlantic Ocean.

Trip to the Airport

e saw the jets come
n. Some jets were
umbo size. One pilot
aved To us. He's a
ice pilot. Maybe
some of us will be
pilots.

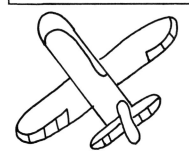

Making Jello
This was fun!
Everybody was
busy mixing
and stirring
and everybody
got to eat.

Trips are so
exciting!
Our trip to
the zoo was
great.
Many animals
came up to us.

The stories may be assembled in chart form and hung on the wall. A coat-and-trouser hanger serves as an excellent holder for the stories. Clothespins also hold the papers together.

PREPARING FOR GROWTH IN WRITTEN EXPRESSION

Working with the type of written expression indicated, the teacher is building an appreciation for the written word, and she is at the same time laying a solid basis for further growth throughout the grades. She is doing her part toward building a wholesome readiness for reading.

GOALS TO BE KEPT IN MIND

A teacher will try:

1. To help the child realize that writing is a means of expression and not an end in itself.

2. To make the child conscious of the fact that the written word serves him and his friends.

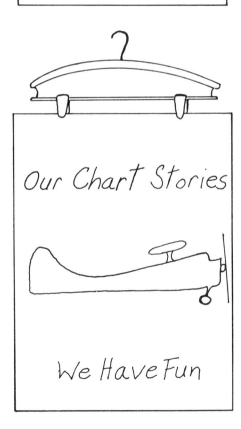

Our Chart Stories

We Have Fun

3. To help the child select the correct way for writing things down, but not to force him.

4. To help him use words that sound pleasant to him and avoid using unpleasant ones.

5. To lead the child slowly into a strong desire to sign his own name, to label some of his belongings, or to write down some of his own ideas.

6. To create in the child a desire for learning to read and write.

DRAMATIZATION

Creative expression and original thinking are vital to the mental and emotional well-being of young children today and may even influence the contributions that they will make to the cultural world of tomorrow.

Perhaps the simplest dramatic experience for the child is *role-playing*. The child actually plays out the role of another person, frequently that of an adult. The role is played as the child sees it, with complete freedom of expression.

Some of the first role-playing takes the form of pantomime —

What am I doing?
Who am I?

It often follows questions such as, "What would you do when Mother says:

'Go to bed now,' or
'Come to dinner'?"

Many inhibitions or aggravations are revealed by enacting roles of parents, brothers and sisters, or friends and playmates.

Recorded conversations are helpful in interpreting behavior. The teacher will be more concerned with the joy of participation than with the perfection of performance. Good interpersonal relationships will be the goal.

Opportunities for interaction are unlimited through dramatic play and creative dramatics. When children on their own play store, house, school, astronauts, etc., and cast themselves as the characters, this is *dramatic play*. Even though it is spontaneous and child initiated, it can be guided so that it too may support intellectual learnings.

Creative dramatics are perhaps the greatest media in this area for furthering language learnings and conceptual growth. The teacher and the children plan and structure roles fully aware of characterization and projection of character traits. Old favorites such as "The Gingerbread Boy," "The Three Bears," and "The Little Red Hen" are good starters. Then stories with more complicated roles can be introduced, planned, and performed. Historical events in which children take the parts are excellent ways to recreate the past. Bible stories with dramatic appeal in which children identify with their favorite characters are powerful character and attitude builders.

All speaking should be free and original, not memorized. Only when a wrong concept is evidenced or distorted language is used should a teacher offer help in choosing terminology.

BUILDING FOUNDATIONS FOR READING

"Learning at any age is successful only when the individual is ready for it."
— *Gertrude Wulfing*

THE KINDERGARTEN PREPARES THE WAY FOR READING

Reading has rightly been called the most important subject in school. It is the foundation of all other schoolwork. Certainly the kindergarten, which lays foundations and builds attitudes, must assume some of the responsibility of preparing children for the great task of learning to read.

READING READINESS — WHAT IS IT?

Perhaps no term has been as misunderstood as the term "reading readiness." It is no subject to be taught in the kindergarten through workbooks, charts, aids, or machines. It is a time — a right time — for teaching; and children arrive at this point at different times. It is an individual matter. One cannot simply say to a child, "Focus your eyes," or "Co-ordinate your muscles," and have it happen; this growth takes time. But it is during this prereading stage that cognitive or intellectual development takes place. When a child is emotionally, socially, mentally, and physically ready, he can learn to read with ease. This is the RIGHT TIME.

Readiness is a continuous process which is governed by the growth pattern of each individual. As children grow in the kindergarten, their language ability grows also. As they approach reading, they need many and varied experiences so they can identify with characters and events in the stories. They need word knowledge, perceptive skills, and healthy bodies and minds to be "ready" for the complex task of learning to read.

Building this readiness takes time, but any structure built for permanency must have a good, solid foundation. So it is with reading.

The teacher will watch for evidences of growth and study each child in the light of his particular experiential background. She will give the children at each stage of growth the richest possible experiences to stimulate them to want to learn, to want to find out, and to want to read. Some will read, and some may have read before they entered kindergarten. However, the success of one or two should not set the standard for the entire group.

CATCH THE SPARK

The discussions as to whether or not reading should be taught in the kindergarten seem to be endless. Both sides present evidence. Research is still going on. Anyone who has worked with boys and girls knows that it is possible to teach reading to children at almost any age, but experts still debate the value rather than the possibility. Research and experience have shown that the age at which a child learns to walk has little to do with his skill in walking later on. So why not let reading come as naturally as walking. Set the stage. When one is ready, let him read. Encourage, but never defeat with practices that may deter rather than accelerate.

The following experiences provide a program for enriching the children's lives and for helping produce reading readiness:

1. Plan short trips and visits to places of interest.

2. Plan social experiences — parties, programs, puppet shows.

3. Provide opportunities for helping with room duties.

4. Plan and play many games to develop cooperation.

5. Provide many opportunities for creative expression.

6. Supply the children picture books and easy reading books.

7. Create a desire to read by reading interesting stories to the children. Have fun.

8. Ask the previous year's kindergarten class to come in occasionally and read to the children.

9. Teach the children how to handle and care for books.

10. Encourage the use of good puzzles.

11. Make use of filmstrips, tapes, overhead projector, and programed learning devices.

12. Plan purposeful activities that will teach children good study habits, and give them many opportunities to grow in all areas of development with continuity and confidence.

In checking the background of experiences that each child possesses, the teacher may ask:

1. Has the child ever traveled? Where? How?

2. What kind of toys does he play with?

3. Has he any books of his own?

4. Do the parents read to him?

5. Does he listen to records? What kind of records?

6. Has he brothers and sisters who play with him?

7. Does the family go to church?

8. Does the family have devotions or prayers together?

9. Has the child a knowledge of pets, plants, animals, transportation, or people of other lands?

The above information can be obtained from conversations with the children and in interviews and visits with the parents, as well as by listening to the children's conversations among themselves.

WATCH FOR PHYSICAL HANDICAPS

A kindergarten teacher will be on guard for any physical handicaps that may retard the child in getting ready to read. She will ask herself these questions:

1. Can the child see things clearly from any part of the room?

2. Can he see things close by?

3. Can he distinguish colors?

4. Does he hear ordinary directions?

5. Does he repeat spoken words correctly?

6. Is he well, or does he show signs of fatigue?

7. Does he hold books at a normal distance from his eyes?

8. Does he have good motor control?

9. Does he notice likenesses and differences in pictures or words?

WATCH FOR MENTAL MATURITY

A child is not ready to read just because

he is six years old chronologically. He must possess a mental maturity that will enable him to cope with the many problems involved in learning to read. A teacher will observe the following:

1. Can the child remember?

2. Is he able to repeat a few sentences after the teacher?

3. Does he try to solve his own little problems?

4. Is he dependent on others for suggestions?

5. Does he have a good speaking vocabulary?

6. Is he able to retell a story in sequence?

7. Is he displaying a normal interest in books?

8. Can he listen attentively?

9. Is he curious when he sees the printed page?

10. Is he familiar with the well-known nursery rhymes and fairy tales?

11. Can he tell a story from a picture?

12. Can he follow simple directions?

WATCH FOR EMOTIONAL MATURITY

Lack of emotional maturity often makes it impossible for children to master skills necessary for reading. They become discouraged at the least little task, have a poor self-image, and give up — defeated before they ever start.

In checking on the socioemotional growth, the teacher will try to find out whether the children are adjusting normally to the situations they meet every day. Some guiding questions may be:

1. Does the child manifest a feeling of security?

2. Is he friendly toward his classmates?

3. Does he mingle with the group, or shy away?

4. Is he overaggressive, bossy?

5. Can he patiently wait his turn?

6. Has he a normal mother-child relationship?

7. Does he seek friends among his classmates, or does he depend on the teacher for friendship?

8. Is he reasonably polite?

9. Can he take a small amount of defeat graciously?

10. Is he able to assume small responsibilities?

11. Does he take correction willingly?

12. Is he becoming conscious of the opinions of others?

13. Does he share?

MULTIPLE ACTIVITIES

The kindergarten teacher will observe the children's total growth patterns while she lives and learns with them during the various activities. She will, through the use of good books and interesting stories, build in them a keen desire to want to read. She will read aloud directions for playing games, perhaps even some simple recipes, to show how people depend on reading in their daily lives.

A kindergarten that is to stimulate children to want to read must have an abundance of good and attractive books, which the children may look at and handle frequently. It must also possess centers of interest, tables and shelves with interesting toys, puzzles, and pictures, so that the children can explore, investigate, question, and learn. A telephone, a dollhouse, a play store, dolls, puppets, and a place to dramatize "made-up" stories all help to foster growth in language.

A post office corner with a mailbox (a shoe box will serve the purpose), into which notes, valentines, birthday invitations, or cards are dropped, serves as an activity that will interest children in reading and in learning how reading and writing serve the community.

A Valentine unit, during which the children mail their own valentines and try to find out who sent them, does a great deal to foster an interest in reading and often in writing.

Let the children live freely, create freely, think freely, and express themselves freely. Then it will be possible for a teacher to study them as individuals and help them grow in each phase according to their particular needs.

ACTIVITIES FOR DEVELOPING VISUAL DISCRIMINATION (Picture Study)

1. Collect pictures from old magazines and sort them according to subject headings, such as: animals, foods, the seasons, people, cars, clothes. Place the pictures on a large piece of beaver board, display board, or large table where children can sort them into proper groupings. After the pictures have been sorted according to proper headings, mix them up again and let another group of children do the sorting. Children will soon see likenesses and differences and grow quite adept in discriminating.

2. Pick out pictures that go together, as:
   a. All the animals that have fur.
   b. All the animals that have claws.
   c. All the animals that give us food.
   d. All the animals that are pets.
   e. All the animals that can climb.

3. Separate pictures of winter clothing and summer clothing; or of objects that move and others that stand still.

4. Have the children pick out two pictures that go together, as:
   a. Socks with shoes.
   b. Cup with saucer.
   c. Coat with hat
   d. Knife with fork.

A list such as the following serves as a guide to observe growth in reading readiness.

BARBE TEACHING SKILLS CHECK LIST
Readiness Level

(last name)	(first name)	(name of school)
(age)	(grade placement)	(name of teacher)

I. VOCABULARY

A. Word Recognition

1. Interested in words ____
2. Recognizes own name in print ____
3. Knows names of letters ____
4. Knows names of numbers ____
5. Can match letters ____
6. Can match numbers ____
7. Can match capital and small letter ____

B. Word Meaning

1. Speaking vocabulary adequate to convey ideas ____
2. Associates pictures to words ____
3. Identifies new words by picture clues ____

II. PERCEPTIVE SKILLS

A. Auditory

1. Can reproduce pronounced two- and three-syllable words ____
2. Knows number of sounds in spoken words ____
3. Can hear differences in words ____
4. Able to hear length of word (Which is shorter? boy-elephant) ____
5. Able to hear sound:
   At beginning of word ____
   At end of word ____
   In middle of word ____
6. Hears rhyming words ____
7. Aware of unusual words ____

B. Visual

1. Uses picture clues ____
2. Recognizes
   Colors ____
   Sizes (big, little; tall, short) ____
   Shapes (square, round, triangle) ____
3. Observes likeness and differences
   in words ____
   in letters ____
4. Left-right eye movements ____

III. COMPREHENSION

A. Interest

1. Wants to learn to read ____
2. Likes to be read to ____
3. Attention span sufficiently long ____

B. Ability

1. Remembers from stories read aloud: ____
   Names of characters ____
   Main ideas ____
   Conclusion ____
2. Can keep events in proper sequence ____
3. Uses complete sentences ____
4. Can work independently for short periods ____
5. Begins at front of book ____
6. Begins on left hand page ____
7. Knows sentence begins at left ____

IV. ORAL EXPRESSION

A. Expresses self spontaneously ____
B. Able to remember five-word sentence ____
C. Able to make up simple endings for stories ____
D. Able to use new words ____

* Reprinted with the permission of the owner of the copyright. Additional copies may be ordered from 3124 Harriet Road, Cuyahoga Falls, Ohio 44224.

5. Have children make their own categories and illustrate.

6. Numbers from large calendars can be cut out and used for sorting and arranging in sets or for playing store.

7. Alphabet cards or old flash cards may be used to match letters or words and to build a story sentence.

8. Cut out mother animals and corresponding baby animals and have the children sort them according to families.

9. Find a few old picture books and cut out the pictures of a story. See if the children can find the picture that would come first in the story, the one that would come next. See if they can follow a sequence in thinking. Place all the pictures in full view so that the children can follow while you tell or read the story.

10. Make ABC booklets with pictures for the various letter sounds.

ACTIVITIES FOR DEVELOPING AUDITORY DISCRIMINATION
(Listening Activities)

1. Use a drum, a triangle, bells, a glass, two pieces of paper, or any other objects that make noise, and have the children become familiar with the different sounds. Then have a child face away and see if he can recognize them.

2. Teach the children the rhythm of various activities such as:

   a. jumping   d. walking   f. clapping
   b. skipping   e. running   g. trotting
   c. hopping

   Have them guess what a child is doing from the sound they hear. One child would perform either in the corridor or while the others have their eyes closed.

3. Have the children listen for words that rhyme. They can at times be asked to

supply the missing word in a poem or jingle, as:

Little Jack Horner
Sat in a _____.

Pitter, patter goes the rain
On the roof and window _____.

4. Let them guess riddles, such as:

I'm thinking of something that sounds like *room* (broom).

I'm thinking of something that sounds like *fall* (ball).

The learning and listening to rhymes and jingles are among the most interesting and effective means of developing auditory discrimination. Children love to hear them over and over again and will soon enjoy substituting the missing words in all their rhymes and poems.

A kindergarten child should be able:

1. To speak in simple, well-constructed sentences.

2. To recognize his own name and some names of his playmates.

3. To repeat about five- or six-word sentences easily.

4. To recognize a few simple words in his environment as: STOP, GO, MOTHER.

5. To recognize the days of the week on a calendar, not by letter form, but by sequence: Sun., Mon., Tues., Wed., Thurs., Fri., Sat.

6. To take part in short dramatizations.

7. To tell a story, or repeat a poem.

8. To notice some differences in sounds (auditory discrimination only).

9. To see likenesses and differences.

10. To anticipate an outcome or next incident in a story.

11. To recognize that information can be gained from books and that reading serves a purpose.

Only when ready, or when feeling the need for it, should the child learn to write his name; then, preferably, with a large crayon.

9. Mathematics

One, two, three, four, five;
I caught a fish alive.
Six, seven, eight, nine, ten;
I let him go again.

EXPLORING MATHEMATICAL CONCEPTS

If children are viewed in the light of their individual growth patterns and varied backgrounds, it is easily understood why some exhibit quite mature mathematical knowledge while others need long periods of carefully planned activities before arriving at the same point of maturity. A kindergarten teacher must help each child move at his own pace in discovering concepts and new relationships in a creative atmosphere.

Perhaps no curriculum area has undergone such a drastic revision as mathematics. Because of recent research, great changes have taken place from the college level down to the preschool years. The emphasis at each stage has been on:

1. discovering ideas
2. seeking relationships
3. developing generalizations.

Children are capable of dealing with mathematical concepts at an earlier age than formerly thought. Since the new emphasis is on developing concepts instead of excellence in computation, one can see how young children would delight in the creative side of mathematics without the fear of failure. "Math" can now become a challenge, an adventure.

CHILDREN ARE INTERESTED IN NUMBERS

Most children have already established a basis for mathematical activities before the age of five. In their play life at home and in the neighborhood they have judged space and distances; they have estimated, counted, and compared. They also have had some experiences with the use and value of money, the importance of time, and the need for numbers in their lives.

In their play one often hears: "I can run *faster* than you," "Let's climb *higher*," and "My daddy's *bigger* than yours." In building they *compare* the blocks they need to make things of various sizes and shapes. They also *count*, *add*, and *subtract* in their own way when building trains or working on other projects. They want to find out *how many more* blocks or cars they need, and often, when playing store, they actually *make change* in their simple but workable way. They weigh, they measure, they evaluate.

The children's daily language reveals how much they know about numbers in general. Their desire to use numbers is a good indication that they are ready to enlarge their concepts and learn even better how numbers may function in their daily lives. Whereas most educators feel there should be no formal period for math instruction, a teacher should plan her day so that the actual teaching of mathematical concepts is developed through incidental, not accidental, experiences. She should provide opportunities to think mathematically and to create ways of attacking problems. If situations and opportunities are provided, most children will discover many mathematical concepts by themselves.

The school day is full of opportunities for stimulating interest in activities that involve number ideas and concepts. When the children play with blocks, they will *measure* them quite accurately to find some that match. One will hear expressions such as: "This block is *longer* than that one," "We need one that is only *half* as long," and "Bring me *two more* long ones." When putting things away, the teacher will encourage the children to put all the blocks that are of *one shape and size* together, perhaps on the shelf that is *lower than the rest*, or on the shelf that is the *widest*.

When playing in the dollhouse, the children have many chances to use number activities. If they build their own playhouse, they will have to do accurate *measuring,* perhaps mostly by direct measuring or *comparison,* but also sometimes by use of a yardstick because they will want to prove their findings. If they should furnish the dollhouse themselves, they will have to *measure* for rugs and curtains and perhaps even for the furniture.

When playing store, children enjoy *making change* and accepting payment for articles. Most children will quite readily recognize a penny, a nickel, and a dime. A little cash register affords both fun and purposeful activity. Small telephones also allow the children to *use numbers* in dialing or calling one another's numbers.

As children use numbers in their activities, they develop their number ideas and concepts quite naturally. They begin to match groups of things and begin to count.

MATCHING SETS

Some have learned to count by rote to 100 but have no understanding of the meaning of such numerals as 4 or 7. "New math" introduces the "set" or the "group" easily so that the cardinal meaning of numerals can be developed through the counting of objects in the various "sets." The child enjoys working with groups or collections of objects and comparing, using such terminology as:

Which set is greater?
Which is lesser?
Are the sets equivalent?

COUNTING AND COMPARING

There are also many opportunities during the day to enumerate things and people. Children enjoy counting the boys and girls that are present and comparing the "sets."

Children can also count when distributing supplies. They may count the children at a particular table or in a special place and provide enough supplies for them. Others can set the lunch table with a cup for each one or a napkin at each chair. They will discover by arranging or rearranging and even locate "empty" situations.

The building of patterns is an activity that can be begun early in their mathematical adventures. The teacher may introduce per-

Correct Figures

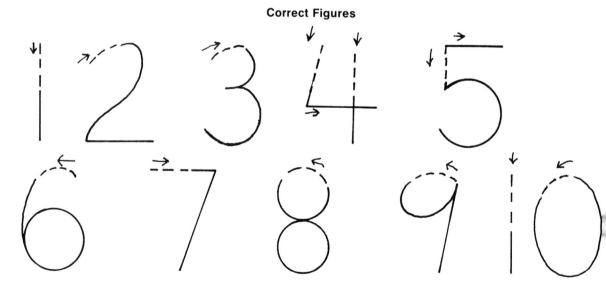

Note: The dots show the child where to start the number

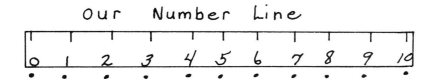

Our Number Line

ceptual cards that show various patterns and interest the children in reproducing them or in making variations.

KEEPING RECORDS

As the children notice that their teacher records their findings, they become interested in keeping records. They begin to want to use number symbols themselves as they play games and keep score. Throwing a ball into a wastepaper basket, ring toss, or bouncing a ball are activities that could require simple keeping of scores on the chalkboard or on a chart.

As children begin to feel the need to write the numerals, the teacher will take every opportunity to call attention to the proper formation of the "figures" as she writes them but will not require any child to write them. If the children start on their own, it is then wise to show them how the figures are formed and to encourage the children to make them correctly. If incorrect writing of the figures

has been learned and made a habit, the children will encounter difficulty in the grades following. The number line should be introduced early and constant use of it encouraged.

NUMBER ACTIVITIES

If some of the children are ready to write the number symbols themselves, they should be given a piece of chalk or a large black crayon. Small-muscle growth should not be forced before the large muscles are strengthened.

Activities other than writing the numerals are of greater value in building math concepts in a kindergarten. Large numbers cut from calendars and pasted on cardboard can be matched with objects on other cards to assist in number values. The teacher can gather any kind of manipulative materials that the children can use to show different one-to-one correspondence. This type of activity is more worthwhile than repetitive drills in formal workbooks.

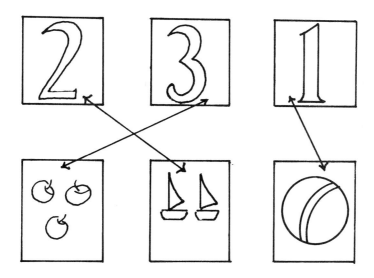

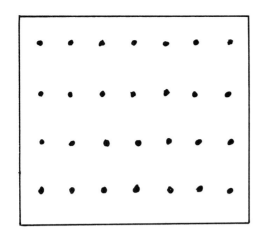

A pegboard is another aid for matching and comparing sets and subsets. Golf tees may be used in the holes.

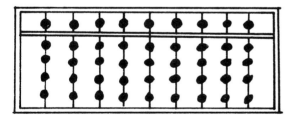

The abacus is valuable in showing the structure of the number system.

An alert teacher will find many interesting ways through which she may help the children with the incidental number experiences such as the counting concept, estimating, recognizing pairs, and sequence of events.

Many materials can be collected at home and brought to school by the children:

bottle caps	egg cartons	plastic straws
boxes	golf tees	small lids
buttons	nails	spools
clothespins	plastic spoons	toothpicks

If one wishes, manipulative materials can be purchased from professional publishers.

A kindergarten classroom should have a variety of materials with which children can play and discover new concepts on their own. A partial list might include:

blocks	puzzles with
clock	geometric designs
colored beads	scales
dominos	tape measure
flannel boards	thermometer
magnets	toy telephones
measuring spoons	yardstick
play money	magnets

CONCEPTUAL LEARNING

Concepts such as larger, smaller, greater, lesser, corner, edge, and side and the meanings of such words as under, between, after, before, behind, top, outside, and bottom can best become a part of the child's vocabulary when he works with objects and derives meaning from his experimentation.

The use of the number line should be introduced to the children to aid them in the personal use of numbers.

Comparison, identification of sets, recognition of shapes, introduction of ordinal numbers, equivalent and nonequivalent sets and subsets all can be introduced by teacher-made charts, which serve as better aids than formal workbooks.

NUMBER CHARTS

Number charts can be easily made by the teacher or by the teacher with the pupils. Use large oak-tag paper or poster paper, and draw, paste, or stencil the numbers on it. The children can draw or cut out pictures to match the numbers.

Simple Concept Charts

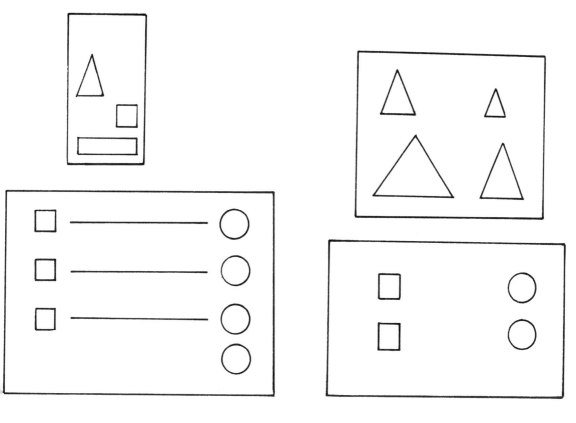

Number Chart

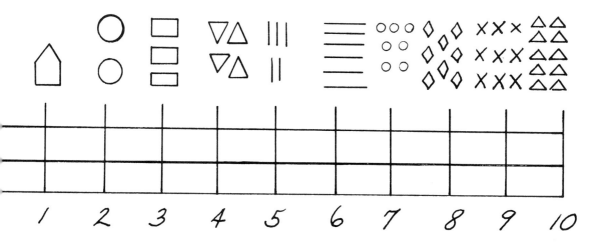

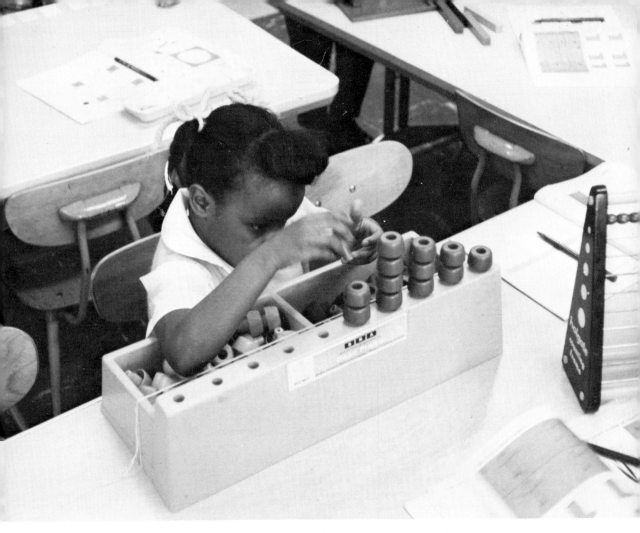

Smaller charts can be made on 9- by 12-inch construction paper if desired. The objects need not be pasted, but the children can arrange them on the correct cards like number puzzles. These charts aid the children in making up their own number stories.

$$2 + \boxed{} = 4$$

$$3 = 1 + \boxed{}$$

$$1 + 1 = \boxed{}$$

$$\boxed{} = 1 + 3$$

How Tall am I?		
	48	Kenny
Christy	47	
Jon	46	
	45	Bob Fred
Sharon	44	Nancy
Irvin	43	
Jim	42	Anne
Walter	41	Jerry
	Inches Measuring Chart	

MEASURING CHART

An activity that invariably fascinates the growing child is keeping a record of his growth. A measuring chart may be hung on the wall where the children can stand and measure themselves. They are delighted to find out how tall they are and how tall their friends are. The inches can be marked in the proper spaces by the teacher, and the children need only stand straight and have one of the others put down a small mark. The teacher can then record the name beside the inch mark. The children may like to put up their own names, which the teacher has previously written on gummed paper.

MONEY VALUES

Money values become real to small children when they begin to use real money. Besides using imitation paper money in their make-believe play in their little store or post office, there will be some opportunities for the children to handle actual coins. The children may have small banks into which they place a few pennies every week. Many of them save for some worthy cause and share in the joy of giving. Some children buy their milk each day or bring money to the teacher for other purposes. The teacher should use such opportunities to show the value of the coins and point out that sometimes a person receives money back because a coin is worth more than the goods that are purchased.

TIME

After children have been in school for a few weeks, they begin to notice the sequence of events during the day. They notice that after they have done one thing for a while, they start something new. They gradually learn that the clock tells them when activities begin and when they stop. The day is beginning to be interpreted as morning, afternoon, and night. The children also begin to realize that the days have names and that the days always come in the same order. Some are school days, one is a play day, and one is the Lord's Day. Sometimes they talk about the

months and years in connection with their ages.

Many games can be played in learning time values:

Guess When

One child will say, "Guess when," and follow this with one of the statements below. Another child will give the right answer.

Guess When—

	Morning	Noon	Night
I go to bed	———	———	———
I eat breakfast	———	———	———
I eat lunch	———	———	———
I get up	———	———	———
It gets dark	———	———	———
My favorite TV program is	———	———	———

Match Me

The teacher or the children may cut out pictures of nighttime, sunsets, children sleeping, snow, harvesttime, falling leaves, or other events indicative of time, and then the children may match them with the time of day or the time of year. When the child holds up a picture, he may say: "When is this?"

The child who guesses correctly may have a turn to hold the picture.

Clock Game

There is never a need to teach kindergarten children to tell time. However, they do enjoy matching the hands on a toy clock with the hands on the real clock at certain times during the day. Children who are ready and feel the need or have a deep interest in time will pick up this sometimes complicated activity.

Clean-Up Time

A three-minute sandglass affords a lot of fun if set for clean-up time. The children quite easily develop the concept of "a few minutes" in which to finish a given task. An alarm clock or timer may also serve as a reminder.

The Calendar

The calendar provides good activity for developing time concepts. The children will enjoy marking off the days as they pass and checking birthdays and special events on them.

WEIGHT

Kindergarten children are delighted when the school nurse or visiting nurse comes into the room and weighs them. They are interested in hearing and comparing how much they weigh in pounds. If there is no nurse to do this, the teacher may quite easily carry on the activity herself with the help of an older pupil or a mother.

From this periodic check on weight an interest in weighing and lifting other things develops. An old scale or balancing board gives pleasure to children who like to gain concrete experience in this skill. The children like to weigh blocks or packages of various sizes, which can be filled with materials or different weights. Beanbags, blocks, and marbles are fun to weigh.

TEMPERATURE

The weather is always a pleasant topic of conversation. Children make comparisons and speak of their feelings of warm and cold. They become interested in the thermometer, and sometimes some of them notice the degrees—hot, cold, freezing, or below zero—and become familiar with the commonly used terms. Occasionally a child may wish to record the temperature in degrees on the Weather Chart or in their chart stories—as "News of the Day."

ALLOW ROOM FOR INITIATIVE

Children themselves will find many ways to use numbers for their own needs and enjoyment, and they should be allowed and encouraged to do so. Caution must be taken not to force children into an unnatural situation to teach them number values and concepts. This may build up a dislike for numbers and inhibit any free exploration, discovery, and evaluation on the children's part.

A teacher will want to become acquainted with concepts of modern mathematics, will use improved teaching techniques, and will alert herself to the latest developments in learning theory.

10. Tell It Again

There are stories of animals,
    Butterflies, bees,
And stories of fairies and elves,
    If you please.
Yes, thousands of stories
    Small children enthrall —
But the stories of Jesus
    Are the best ones of all.

OBJECTIVES OF STORYTIME

1. To develop a love for literature in the child.

2. To help the child stimulate his thinking into creative channels.

3. To develop the imagination.

4. To give delightful experiences to the children.

5. To stimulate the child to express his feelings through art and activity.

6. To lead to a desire to dramatize experiences.

7. To develop good listening habits.

8. To build up a repertoire of good, interesting stories.

9. To help the child understand better and more fully the problems of other people.

10. To develop a desire to learn to read.

CHILDREN LOVE STORIES

Happy are the children who can gather around a Christian teacher and hear the most wonderful of all stories — the real, true stories of Jesus. Use these stories in your storytime hour also, even though you teach them more fully in your "Christian Living and Learning" activities. The children will never tire of them, and they will be happy to know Bible heroes such as David, Daniel, and Joseph, as well as their heroes drawn from other sources.

Reading and telling stories are two of the essential foods for the creative life of children. Lead the children carefully into the fascinating realms of "storybook land," into the world of make-believe at first, and then also into the great ocean of knowledge that can be reached by reading good books.

A small child's spirit is easily accessible and requires little to bring it out to a full response. Few audiences are more responsive to stories than a group of little boys and girls — all eyes on you, eager to listen.

WHY HAVE STORYTIME?

1. Children love stories. They love to have them read or, even better, told to them.

2. Stories help children feel the beauty of language and thrill of communication.

3. They serve as an introduction to good literature.

4. They serve a definite purpose in —
   a. answering questions.
   b. stimulating ideas.
   c. giving correct information.
   d. teaching a truth.
   e. providing real joy.

THE TEACHER SHOULD RECOGNIZE THE VALUE OF GOOD STORIES

A teacher must recognize the important part the telling and reading of stories and poetry plays in the language arts program. She knows the joys that good children's literature brings and the vital part it plays in the imaginative and creative life of children. Sharing literature with the children is one of the more important ways to strengthen their communicative skills.

Although children enjoy having stories read to them as well as told to them, a good storyteller is a favorite with young children. A little practice can make a teacher an expert in telling stories artfully and effectively.

HOW TO TELL A STORY

When telling a story, it is wise to have it very well prepared, with the direct quotations memorized. Many stories depend entirely on

direct discourse to make the story complete. When the occasion permits, the storyteller may feel free to add interesting new descriptions and words. This often puts special magic in the air. Children, too, may wish to make special endings for the stories. This stimulates imagination. A teacher who is enthusiastic about a story will generally be able to arouse the enthusiasm of the children.

SELECTION IS IMPORTANT

There are literally thousands of children's books on the market today, and the selection of worthwhile material becomes a challenge. Published lists assist in the selection. Be sure that the librarian is a friend of yours, and use her and her special talents when choosing books for your library center.

Most children like the story hour, so have a variety of books—for information, for recreation, for aesthetic enjoyment (poetry). Stories in which children are the main characters, animal stories, fairy tales, stories with surprises and with fast-moving plots are among the children's favorites.

Because of the great challenge in selecting worthwhile books for young children, a few excellent sources ought to be made available to every teacher. Some that might prove helpful in selecting children's literature are:

Arbuthnot, May Hill, et al. *Children's Books Too Good to Miss.* Cleveland: Press of Case-Western Reserve University, 1966.

Crosby, Muriel, ed. *Reading Ladders for Human Relations.* Washington, D. C.: American Council on Education, 1963.

Hollowell, Lillian, ed. *A Book of Children's Literature.* New York: Holt, Rinehart, and Winston, Inc., 1966.

SOME THINGS TO REMEMBER
FOR THE STORY HOUR

1. When first selecting a story to read or tell, choose a short one, one that takes no longer than several minutes. As a rule use only one story to leave the children with one impression. Do not choose a story that has to be continued until they have matured a little.

2. Choose stories with good illustrations and show the pictures to the group.

3. Frequently select stories in which the children can join in the refrain, supply details, or rhyming words. They like to participate.

4. When choosing stories, look for simplicity, sincerity, and spontaneity.

5. Include in your selections samplings of folk, realistic, and modern fanciful tales. Try to maintain a balance of factual and fanciful tales to help the children gradually distinguish between truth and fiction.

6. Enjoy the story yourself. Show your feelings as you read or tell it. Children catch your spirit readily. So do not come with a "poker face" and then expect the children to enjoy the story.

7. Expect a courteous, attentive attitude from your children but allow for a relaxed position and a feeling of well-being. Deliberate distractions need correction.

8. Keep your voice pleasant and conversational. Avoid nasality. Change the inflection and tempo frequently.

9. Let your children react to the stories through music, art, dramatic play, and free conversation.

STORIES ENCOURAGE EXPRESSION

Stories lend themselves beautifully to a natural growth in the art of expression. Children should not only be encouraged to react and speak freely, but should also be encouraged to tell their "made-up" stories to the group and feel free to use them in their dramatic play. They should also be encouraged to choose stories for the storytime period.

Do not always plan your story hour by the clock, but bring in your stories at various intervals during the day. In this way they become spontaneous expressions and the happy medium to introduce children to the tremendous field of good literature.

11. Play Activities

Girls and boys are bright and gay!
Life for them is mostly play—
And they think it so much fun,
Just to jump and skip and run.

OBJECTIVES

1. To provide the children with large muscle activity through games and exercises.

2. To help the children develop the ability to play together in small groups.

3. To teach children the need for fair play and for taking turns.

4. To teach them how to use play apparatus properly and creatively.

5. To show them the need for outdoor activity.

6. To develop a feeling for and an appreciation of rhythm and imitative activities.

7. To teach children to follow simple directions.

8. To teach them to share playground toys with others.

9. To teach children that playing cooperatively is treating playmates and friends with kindness.

10. To help them realize that it is fun to play with enthusiasm, even games that they may not choose or wish to play.

11. To help children learn that it is fun to play, regardless of who wins the game.

12. To help them find real joy in vigorous activity.

PLAY IS NATURAL

Play is the natural expression of childhood. It contributes greatly to the social, emotional, physical, and intellectual well-being of the child. Little children should have from four to five hours of large muscle activity each day, ample time for free play alone or in small groups, and time for some rhythmical and developmental activities. Play is to chil-

dren what work is to adults. It is essential to their growth and development. In fact, they cannot grow without it. It is the one activity in which all children love to participate regardless of age, size, or maturity. Here individual differences and preferences can be properly taken into account.

THE TEACHER AS A GUIDE

The play period should be a period of good fun and comradeship, to which the teacher lends added enjoyment by joining wholeheartedly in the activities. She is one of the group, but she is the most mature, the one best fitted to lead and guide. Any play period must be under the careful and skillful planning and execution of the teacher. Uncontrolled, boisterous, disorderly play has no place in a kindergarten where children are learning the first courtesies of Christian living together. It should not be forgotten that the play period is also a learning experience.

The children at times enjoy choosing their own games to play, and this is desirable if the teacher does not leave it to casual and random choosing. She will still guide and suggest games that will be enjoyable and profitable for all. She can do this by limiting the selection to a few games and by quite frequently making the choice herself.

Through play a child—

Explores his own strengths.
Experiments with ways of doing things.
Repeats performance to practice skills.
Builds social relationships and makes judgments.
Attempts to solve problems.

FREE PLAY

A period of free play usually begins when the children arrive at school. Each child is encouraged to choose his own toy, equipment, or materials with which he wishes to play. At first he may wish to play by himself or he may be satisfied just to be an onlooker. A normal reaction will then be to become a cooperative member of a play group. This will come gradually with some children. The teacher will carefully guide the play of the very shy and of the overstimulated or selfish child. She will be at hand to give help when it is needed.

The free-play period offers an excellent opportunity to care for the individual needs of the children. Levels of motor development and individual differences will necessitate a variety of activities. Some children will prefer to play with constructive toys—building barns, farms, and houses. Others will want action—moving toys, trucks, and trains. Still others prefer the quiet, imaginary games, telephoning and dollhouses, while another group may be happy to engage in dramatic play, the "make-believe." Some will prefer to use magnets, tools, science equipment, records, filmstrips, or puzzles. Provision should be made for all kinds of activities.

During this time the teacher indirectly guides the free play. This is a time when children learn to play cooperatively, respecting the rights and wishes of others. The child who cannot work with his hands to make things may be skillful in using the apparatus, in tumbling on mats, or in playing with large balls. The child who cannot paint or draw well may be a good leader for games and rhythms. The free period is one of the best times to encourage Christian living among the boys and girls.

When the free-play period is over, all equipment should be put away carefully and neatly by the children. Habits of orderliness are begun in the play period. Enough time should be allowed for cleaning up and putting away, and a gong or a chord on the piano can serve as a gentle reminder that in a few minutes the toys will all be put away.

There should be a place for everything, and the spaces should be large enough to store games and equipment without crowding or piling one on top of the other.

A few well-chosen, sturdy toys and games are better than many cheap, easily broken ones.

It is wise to vary the toys occasionally. Some can be packed away for future use. This procedure will keep the room spacious and free for play, and at the same time it induces the child to appreciate an orderly room. A crowded room becomes a cluttered room and tends to confuse children who are learning the first principles of neatness and order.

Equipment for free play will vary according to available space. The following items of play equipment are suggested:

Balls—large rubber or stuffed balls for bouncing, rolling, and throwing.

Beanbags—these may be homemade. They can be used in place of balls for tossing to each other or for tossing into the beanbag board.

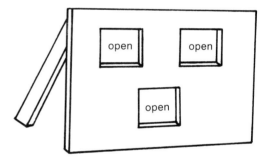

Beanbag Board

Blocks—large blocks for building. Hollow blocks are easily handled and can be made of balsa wood or bought commercially.

A Dollhouse—this can be made from an orange crate or bought. It should be as large as the room will permit.

Ropes—for jumping.

Toy Animals and a Barn.

Puzzles—with degrees of difficulty since some children are very adept at this skill.

Sandbox and Tools — if space permits.

A Tricycle — if the room is large or if there is an outdoor play space.

Planks.

Wagons or Carts.

Dolls — rag dolls, paper dolls, and dolls for the playhouse.

Musical Toys — xylophone, cymbals, bells, triangle, drums, tambourines.

Geometric Shapes.

Magnets.

Beads and Pegs.

Pegboards.

Tops.

A Ladder.

Picture Lotto.

Picture Dominoes.

Record Player — preferably unbreakable records so that the children can play them by themselves.

Pictures — all kinds to cut out and paste.

Walking Boards.

Small Cars; Airplanes; Trucks; Boats; and **Small Wooden, Plastic,** or **Rubber People.**

Ring Toss or **Horseshoe Game.**

Ten Pins.

Jump Ropes.

Dramatic Play Equipment.

STORY PLAYS

Story plays differ from dramatic plays in that all the children in story plays do all the acting together, whereas there may be many separate roles enacted in dramatic play.

The teacher usually introduces the play with several suggested sentences, and as the children become experienced, they will add their own ideas. The best story plays are an outgrowth of the experiences the children have had. A few examples are described to serve as models.

Autumn in the Woods

1. Trip to the woods — walk or ride bus.
2. Skip and shuffle through the leaves.
3. Gather up leaves into a big pile.
4. Jump into the pile of leaves.
5. Look into the trees for birds' nests.
6. Run and jump over a stream in the woods.
7. Throw stones into the water.
8. Pick apples in an orchard.

Playing in the Snow

1. Dress to go outdoors — scarfs, mittens, boots.
2. Walk through deep snow — legs up high.
3. Roll big snowballs to make a fort.
4. Pile on more snow.
5. Pat it down hard.
6. Snowball fight — all make snowballs. Then one half throw at the others, who dodge the snowballs.
7. Repeat — the other side dodging and the second side throwing.
8. Walk home through deep snow.
9. Take in deep breaths of fresh air.
10. Undress.

Firemen

1. Firemen asleep — heads on table.
2. Fire bell rings — all jump up and dress while on the run.
3. Jump on truck and drive to fire — stationary running steps (sirens).
4. Unwind hose — hands clasped together.
5. Grasp hoses — squirt streams of water from side to side and up and down.

6. Raise ladders—pull on rope to raise ladder.

7. Climb up ladders.

8. Bring out people and valuable things.

9. Climb down ladder—using one hand only.

10. Wind hose and put back on truck.

11. Drive slowly home.

12. Undress and go back to bed or sit down to eat.

GAMES

Fresh air, sunshine, open spaces, and physical activity are conducive to the health and happiness of children. An outdoor period of play offers the greatest opportunity for activity and enjoyment and gives the children an opportunity to release some of the abundant energy stored up in their growing bodies.

The five-year-old, an active, growing, changing being, simply cannot sit still long. He is happiest when he is running, jumping, wriggling, or chasing around. So let him play out of doors if the weather permits, otherwise in the kindergarten room or in the gymnasium.

A healthy play program presupposes that a kindergarten room has enough open space to allow the children to play freely, or that the children have access to larger places for active play.

Most of the games suggested will lend themselves both to indoor and outdoor play.

Some kindergarten teachers have discarded group games, feeling that they are too highly organized for small children. Although young children are happy to play in smaller groups, they also enjoy the active and imaginative larger group games. Through such activity they learn cooperation, emotional stability, physical coordination, and acceptable Christian social behavior, which builds a feeling of belonging and confidence in their own ability. The teacher, however, will select simple games and give only a few directions. She will introduce games that will capture the children's interest and meet their needs and abilities. She will also change games frequently and see to it that all children participate.

TEACH CHILDREN TO TAKE TURNS

Small children cannot wait long for turns. When choosing some of the circle games, it is a good idea to have several circles playing at the same time, particularly if the group is large. A child that has been chosen for a second turn before all have had a turn could be taught to say, "I've had a turn," and choose another child. This is demonstrating a Christian principle of love and consideration, and children enjoy choosing one another.

USE SIMPLE GAMES

Many of the traditional games, such as "London Bridge" and "Drop the Handkerchief," can be simplified and easily adapted to small children. It is not wise to change the game itself but merely to choose one or two of the main characteristics and leave the harder parts to the six- and seven-year-olds. The more mature children, then, will have nothing to unlearn but will merely add more parts to the games they already know.

All rules should be simple and carefully stated and then made easy to follow. Observance of the simple rules and directions is good for the social, mental, and physical development of the kindergarten child. However, no penalty should be given for forgetting the rules and making a mistake. Sometimes it is good to separate a small group and first demonstrate the game with a few pupils, so that games become fun and not hard tasks.

To have a game period function, one must remember to keep it on the children's level. Children should not be expected to come up to adult standards of performance.

If a child were to perform according to a finished ideal, his high standard of performance would likely be the direct result of superimposed perfection, and this is undesirable. This type of performance would have no educational value for the children engaged in it but would merely gratify the desire of the teacher to have her group excel in standards that she herself has imposed arbitrarily.

To guide children in play, the teacher needs an intelligent and sympathetic insight into the many activities of children and a keen understanding of their ways of doing things. Through careful planning and sincere encouragement, she can then slowly lead them into better ways of playing, remembering that play is the child's life, which he must live happily and successfully.

STANDARDS FOR SELECTING GAMES

The following points may be helpful in selecting and directing games:

1. Select games that interest the children.

2. Know the game thoroughly before you try to play it.

3. Let the play spirit prevail; enjoy the game yourself.

4. Make rules the children can understand, and then follow them with patience.

5. Encourage courtesy and consideration at all times.

6. Discourage all unnecessary shouting and screaming.

7. Avoid competition—the children are not ready for it.

8. Choose games in which all can participate—children would rather participate than watch.

9. Avoid overstimulation and fatigue.

10. Stop the game before interest lags.

11. Watch carefully for fairness.

12. Encourage joyous exuberance, but do not permit rowdiness or hurting one another.

13. Establish the need for the word "stop" or "wait" and seek to get a quick response when it is given. A whistle, a horn, or a chord on the piano helps greatly, especially out of doors.

14. If necessary, stop the game to discuss rules or ways of improving it, especially if disturbance is spoiling the game. If you must eliminate the offender, do it for a short time only. Bring him back for the next game.

15. Praise the children often for their good efforts and their fair play.

16. Provide for frequent repetition of games. Children love to play games that are familiar to them.

17. Maintain a friendly, orderly atmosphere. The happiest play usually goes hand in hand with good discipline. Play is not nervous excitement, but rather orderly, joyous activity.

18. Let the children share in planning the games and occasionally in giving directions and executing them. If children are familiar with certain games, they may well help the teacher in teaching them.

19. Do not expect all children to understand the rules until the game has been played many times.

20. Remember that little children are inexperienced at game organization and have very short interest spans. Plan the games accordingly, and simplify if necessary.

Some games that little children enjoy are listed here. This list is by no means all-inclusive, but it should give the kindergarten teacher an insight into the types of games children enjoy.

ACTIVE GAMES

Follow the Leader

The children form a circle with one child being the leader. The leader chooses an activity, does it, and the group follows. It is advisable to change leaders often.

May We Walk Across the River?

The group forms a straight line, and the teacher stands opposite the line. Two or three are chosen as catchers and are placed in the center, between the group and the teacher. The group calls, "May we walk across the river?" Whereupon the teacher chooses a color and answers, "Yes, but only those who have red on." The children who have red walk across and cannot be caught, while all others have to run across so that they are not caught. The catchers can catch only those who do not have the chosen color. Change colors often and watch to see that everyone gets a chance to have the "safe" colors once in a while. The children who are caught help catch the others.

Chickens, Come Home

The children are formed in a straight line with several children (foxes) in the foreground. A child is chosen for the Mother Hen, who stands opposite the line. She calls out, "Chickens, come home." The chickens in the line call out, "No, Mother, we can't come home." Mother Hen calls again, "You *must* come home." The chickens must then all run, and the foxes in the center run to catch them. Those caught before they reach the opposite side become foxes and help catch the rest of the chickens.

Drop the Handkerchief

This popular game can be adapted in many ways to suit the maturity of the group. The teacher will have to make her own rules to suit the particular group she is teaching. This game can also be played sitting down, since little children tire easily if standing too long without activity. One child may go around the circle tapping the children's head, saying, "Duck, Duck," and when he wants someone to chase him, he adds, "Gray Duck," starts running, and says, "Duck, Duck, Duck, Gray Duck."

Cat and Mouse

The children form a circle with hands clasped and arms raised. A "cat" is on the outside and a "mouse" in the center. On the words, "Mouse, mouse, get out of your house," said by the group, the mouse runs out and the cat immediately after it, chasing around and under the upraised arms of the circle, ducking in and out. When the mouse is caught, the group claps, and another mouse and cat are chosen. The children are to run *under* the arms and must never be allowed to try to jump over or to break through.

Squirrel in the Tree

The simplest form of this game is to have the children divided into groups of three. Two form the tree by clasping hands, and the other one gets in the center of the small circle. The groups are placed around the gymnasium or play yard. Several squirrels are left on the outside without a tree, and at a given signal (a whistle, a chord on the piano, or a clap of the hands), all squirrels must change their places—they must find another tree. The squirrels on the outside have a chance now to find a home, and the ones left without a home wait for the next signal.

Fire Engine

The children form a long line facing front. They are each given a number to remember: usually one, two, three, four. The teacher or a chosen child stands opposite the group and calls interchangeably, "Fire Engine No. 3," or other number, mixing them up frequently. The number called runs across, touches the goal line and returns. Then another number is called. The Chief who calls at times intersperses, "Fire Engine No. False Alarm," when nobody is to run. Or, "Fire Engine No. General Alarm," when all must run. No one catches. The fun is in the running to put out the fire and home again.

Other Games

Dodge Ball, Pussy Wants a Corner, Two Deep, Charlie over the Water, and **Red Light.**

QUIET GAMES

There are times when quiet, relaxing games are appropriate in the kindergarten. However, these games should never take the place of the play activities in which children must participate daily but are to serve as an added activity when tension arises or when children become overstimulated.

Huckle, Buckle, Beanstalk

This is a variation of *Hide the Thimble*. Several children are chosen to leave the room or to hide their eyes while one member of the class hides an object—a ball, a top, or a small toy—anywhere in the room, within sight of all but fairly well concealed. A doorkeeper is chosen, who invites the group in to hunt the object. The hunters must keep their hands behind their backs while hunting. When one child finds the object, he or she walks quietly to his seat and says, "Huckle, buckle, beanstalk." The rest of the children keep on hunting and follow the same procedure until all have found the object. The first finder becomes the hider, and the second finder the doorkeeper. A time limit may be put on the game to prevent stalling.

Doggie, Doggie, Who Has Your Bone?

One child representing the dog sits on a small chair with his eyes closed. Another child creeps up slowly with an object representing a bone and says, "Doggie, who has your bone?" The dog tries to guess from the voice of the child. A variation would be to have the child knock at the chair. The one on the chair would then say, "Who's that knocking at my door?" and the child who knocked would answer, "It is I. It is I," and the child again would try to guess.

Riddle Riddle Ree or Color Game

A child chooses an object in the room and whispers it to the teacher to forestall unfair play. Then the child says:

> "Riddle, riddle, ree,
> I see something you don't see.
> The color of it is _____."

The child who guesses takes a turn.

Meow, Meow

A "mother cat" is chosen. She leaves the room while the teacher taps a few children on the head. These become the lost kittens. All children place their heads on the tables and pretend to sleep. When the mother cat comes home, she has to find her little lost kittens. The children who have been tapped say very softly, "Meow, meow," while the rest keep perfectly still. The mother cat moves about slowly trying to locate her kittens. When she finds one, she calls out its name, and when all are found, another mother cat is chosen.

The kittens may also be hidden around the room and the mother cat blindfolded. In this case the mother cat would merely have to locate the kittens and not be expected to name them.

NOTE—When blindfolding the children, use a clean cloth or towel and line it each time with a clean piece of facial tissue to prevent possible spread of infection.

Guess What

This is a simplified form of *Charades,* where a group may act out a story or an incident, and the rest guess. Bible stories lend themselves well to this type of activity. Examples: Noah Building the Ark. Peter Throwing Out His Nets.

NOTE—Children must not be allowed to become frivolous or disrespectful during this type of game.

Simon Says, "Thumbs Up"

Simon says: Stand up.
Simon says: Jump up.
Simon says: Sit.
Simon says: Stretch.
Simon says: Wave your arms.
One child gives the directions; the others act them out.

Other Games

Everything That Has Feathers Flies
Button, Button, Who Has the Button?
Imaginary Hide and Go Seek

THE USE OF MUSIC RHYTHMS

Rhythms taught and developed during the music activities will be used in many of the games, and from these rhythm activities balance, control, expression, and happy participation can develop. The small child's progress in rhythm activities will depend on his muscular coordination, self-confidence, and ability to interpret his feelings with bodily movement. Through the games the teacher will create situations where the same movements must be used in a variety of ways.

SKIPPING

Many kindergarten children have not yet learned how to skip. Every effort should be made for them to acquire this little skill as soon as possible, for many plays and games require skipping rhythms. Most children pick it up quite naturally. Some learn by going along with the others, but others need definite teaching. When teaching, see that the child knows what a skip is—a step and then a hop, transferring the weight from one leg to the other on the hop. Encourage those having difficulty to say out loud, "Step, hop; step, hop." If the teacher supports the child a little and encourages him, he will soon understand the process.

RHYTHM ACTIVITIES
FOR THE ROOM OR GYMNASIUM

Find appropriate activities that the children enjoy, choose appropriate music, and let the children act them out according to the rhythm. Suggestions:

Mother	Father
Sweeping	Driving a car
Washing dishes	Digging a garden
Dusting	Cutting grass
Ironing	Washing a car
Sewing	Raking leaves
Mending	Playing golf
Baking	Fishing

Mailman	The Farmer
Sorting out mail	Milking the cows
Filling the bag	Driving a tractor
Putting the mail	Picking fruit
in the box	Feeding animals
	Riding a horse

One child may perform and the others guess. The one who guesses correctly would then perform with another activity. Or the class may be divided into groups, and the group would put on the act for the other groups to guess.

After a child or a group has selected an activity, the selection should be told to the teacher to avoid any unfair play, for instance, changing the activity as soon as a certain dominating child guesses, or giving a special friend an advantage. Whispering to the teacher the activity chosen will safeguard any such temptations and will also give the teacher a chance to give guidance and direction when necessary.

Oh, See the Animals in the Zoo!

Little boys and girls will enjoy acting as zoo or circus animals with or without music. The children may be divided into different groups of animals and pretend they are in cages, or they may just form a circle and come forward when it is their turn to perform.

They may sing (to the tune of "Mulberry Bush") and march around the room:

"Oh, see the animals in the zoo,
    In the zoo,
    In the zoo.
All of them different things can do
    And we can do them also."

The children will then act out the next stanzas:

"The elephant walks and swings his trunk,
    Swings his trunk,
    Swings his trunk.
The elephant walks and swings his trunk,
    And we can do it also.

"Oh, see the snake go twisting about,
    Twisting about,
    Twisting about.
Oh, see the snake go twisting about,
    And we can do it also."

The children can add stanzas of their own and act accordingly.

Flop

The children may be directed to run about

the room in an orderly fashion, while the teacher plays the piano or a record. When the music stops, the children flop on the floor. The last one to flop is out and sits on the sidelines, while the game continues. It is played until all but one have been eliminated.

This game teaches a quick reaction and also develops a sense of fair play, for if a child flops before the music stops, he is automatically eliminated.

OTHER ACTIVITIES

A favorite game is to have the children form a circle with one child in the center. This child chooses an activity, and the group marches around him, singing to the tune of "Here We Go Round the Mulberry Bush":

"Bobby [or whatever the child
    may be named],
Tell us what to do,
What to do,
What to do.
Bobby, tell us what to do,
Tell us what to do."

Bobby then tells the activity, and the children go around the circle performing to the music for "Mulberry Bush." After several times around, another child is chosen to call for another activity. Some favorite activities are listed below. The music for most of them is found in *Rhythms for Children*, by Mary S. Shafer and Mary M. Mosher, published by A. S. Barnes and Company, New York.

Marching	Walking like
Skipping	elephants
Running	Waddling like ducks
Trotting	High-stepping ponies
Hopping	Jumping frogs
Jumping	Riding a bicycle
Galloping	Driving a car
Tiptoeing	Piloting a plane
Hopping on one foot	Going into space
Flying like birds	Riding a horse
Walking like	Sliding down
turtles	a fire pole

147

The above activities may also be acted out to records. The teacher asks the children if they can tell what the music sounds like or if they would like to do what the music tells them. Children will differ in their interpretation, and no effort should be made to have them conform too closely to a set pattern. Let them exercise their creative spirit. Some children will be quick to catch the rhythm. Others may be willing to follow. Growth in leadership takes time.

Little encouragements will help the child interpret the rhythm and develop a liking for it. A child with a poor sense of rhythm may be absorbed in a group of better performers and will be content to follow their directions and increase his sensibility without too much concern and worry on his part. A sensitive child often dislikes to act alone but will perform quite well in a group.

SINGING GAMES

Playing and singing are favorite activities in the life of a child. So it is quite natural that when the two activities are combined, they will bring added joy to the children who engage in them.

Since small children cannot stay with one activity for any length of time, it is wise to change activities often or to intersperse them with a good stretch, some exercise, or finger-play.

The teacher and the children may wish to create some of their own games and use them with music or singing. This is a worthwhile activity and should be encouraged.

FINGER PLAYS

The following "Finger Plays" have proved to be fun for the children and are listed to give ideas to those who may wish to make up some more. Suitable actions are suggested by the words.

I'll measure my arms,
I'll measure my nose,

I'll measure myself
From my head to my toes.

Ten little men to market go,
Thumbkins go to buy some meat,
Pointers go to buy some wheat,
Tall men go to carry back
Great big bundles in the sack,
Ring men go to buy some silk,
Babies go to buy some milk.

This is the beehive;
Where are the bees?
Hidden away
Where nobody sees,
Soon they'll come
Creeping out of their hive—
One, two, three, four, five.

This is mother,
This is father,
This is brother tall,
This is sister,
This is baby,
Jesus loves us all.

This is my right hand,
Raise it up high.
This is my left hand,
Twirl them around.
Left hand, right hand,
Pound, pound, pound.

Two little feet go tap, tap, tap,
Two little hands go clap, clap, clap,
One little leap up from the chair,
Two little arms reach high in the air,
Two little feet go jump, jump, jump,
Two little hands go thump, thump, thump,
One little child turns round and round,
One little child sits quietly down.

Left foot, right foot, hear the drum,
Left foot, right foot, tum, tum, tum.
Left foot, right foot, marching feet,
Left foot, right foot, up the street.

Open, shut them [hands],
Open, shut them,

Give a little clap,
Open, shut them,
Open, shut them,
Lay them in your lap.

A little ball [thumb and front finger],
A large ball [fingers],
A great big ball I see [arms];
Now let's count the balls we've made,
One, two, three.

The animals went for a walk one day,
And each one went a different way:
The frisky *squirrels* ran so fast
You scarcely saw them as they passed.
The *elephant* came with a heavy tread,
Swinging and swaying and nodding his head.
The *bob-tailed rabbit* went hoppity, hop,
And his great long ears went flippity, flop.
The *rooster* held his head on high
And flapped his wings as if to fly.
The barnyard *ducklings* waddled with snap
On their short legs and said, "Quack, quack."

When I am big, I feel so tall [stretch high].
When I am little, I feel so small [squat low].
Taller, taller, taller [come up slowly],
Smaller, smaller, smaller [go down slowly],
Till there's nothing left at all [go way down].

If you fold your hands to pray
In this special sort of way,
You'll forget about your play
And remember what you say.

Before my little prayers are said,
I'll fold my hands and bow my head;

I'll try to think to whom I pray,
And try to mean the words I say.

We fold our hands that we may be
From all our work and play set free.
We bow our heads as we draw near
The King of kings, our Savior dear.
We close our eyes that we may see
Nothing to take our thoughts from Thee,
　　　As we pray: Our Father, etc.

Two eyes to see nice things to do,
Two lips to smile the whole day through,
Two ears to hear what others say,
Two hands to put the toys away,
A tongue to speak sweet words each day,
A loving heart to work and play,
Two feet that errands gladly run,
These make good days for everyone.

I can stand on my toes
And make myself tall.
I can bend my knees
And make myself small.
I can make myself tall,
I can make myself small,
I like my own size
　　　Best of all.

Clap your hands so gaily, gaily, gaily,
Clap your hands so gaily, clap, clap, clap.
Swing your arms —
Snap your fingers —
Pound your hands —
Stamp your feet —
Now sit down —
Fold your hands.

12. Healthful Living

HEALTHFUL LIVING AND LEARNING

As one thinks of the health of a young child, one considers not only his physical well-being but his mental and emotional health as well. In this high-powered, competitive culture, a small child's personal world must be a place in which his inner self can gain strength through warm and wholesome relationships. It should be a place where he feels secure, valued, and wanted.

A teacher must be aware of the vital part that her personality, her outlook, her philosophy, and her attitude play in building a healthy mental outlook in her children. For an adequate emotional development a child needs acceptance, approval, and affection from his teacher. Basking in such an atmosphere, a child learns to trust and believe in those who care for him.

An environment filled with the tender love of the Savior reflected in the attitude of the teacher is as important as the physical and personal aspects of health education.

Good health habits would quite naturally grow in this classroom climate. Parents should be aware of the health habits being taught at school, so that through their cooperation the child may more readily accept the standards set for them.

SOME HABITS OF HEALTHFUL LIVING

1. Covering coughs and sneezes.
2. Using tissues properly.
3. Playing outdoors daily.
4. Washing hands when necessary.
5. Dressing appropriately for the weather.
6. Keeping feet dry.
7. Eating proper foods.
8. Keeping fingers away from nose and mouth.
9. Resting when tired.
10. Getting enough sleep.
11. Building good attitudes toward doctors, dentists, and nurses.
12. Appreciating the five senses.
13. Caring for the teeth.

In a health program the teacher must be alert to the many opportunities for learning experiences and concept building that exist. She will also safeguard the health of the children by being a keen observer of early signs of an oncoming illness such as:

running nose	flushed face
weariness	irritability
coughing	crying
sneezing	rubbing eyes
rash	paleness

SNACK TIME SERVES A PURPOSE

The midmorning lunch period or refreshment time is desirable from the standpoint both of social living and of health. It affords the children a natural opportunity to cultivate and to exercise proper attitudes and common courtesies, and it provides some extra lunch for those children who ate only a very light breakfast or perhaps no breakfast at all.

There are numerous ways in which the snacks may be served. This will depend much on the local facilities.

A little cart, gaily painted, or a wagon may be used to distribute milk cartons to the children at the tables. The milkman may even wear a white coat or hat. This procedure will definitely encourage the children to find their places and remain orderly while being served.

Little helpers may be chosen to hand out the napkins. Cut large napkins in four pieces for the small children. A piece six or eight inches square is large enough for them—and you will save on the napkins. Others may pass the crackers or other food. Helpers should be chosen anew each day so that all children receive frequent turns and many different experiences.

FRIENDLY HELPERS CHART

A "Friendly Helpers" chart may be hung up and the names of the helpers posted every day. The name of "friendly helper" or "little helper" is far more appropriate than the mature expression of host or hostess, which is sometimes used.

Friendly Helpers Chart

Since not all the children will finish at the same time, those who finish first should be asked to remain at their seats and wait a reasonable time for the others. When most have finished, the teacher rings a bell or chime to signal cleanup time. Each child should feel a personal responsibility to put his carton in the cart or box and clean up his part of the table. A few small wastepaper baskets are better than one big one. A large soft sponge is an ideal help for wiping up spilt milk or juice. It absorbs readily and makes it easy for the children to clean up their own "spill." When everything is cleaned up, the children may gather around for a story or get ready for the rest period. While the children wait for others to finish eating, they may engage in conversation with one another. The time could also be used for sharing or reporting time. This can be an added "fun" time.

CONVERSATION WHILE EATING

During the lunch period, however, the children should be encouraged to carry on controlled conversation with one another, tell stories or riddles, and enjoy a period of relaxation, which should never become boisterous or rude. Loud talking and fighting or throwing of food should be discouraged.

PRAYER AT MEALTIME

The table prayer may be selected and led by a child, if he so desires. The child or the teacher may wish to say:

"Let us fold our hands and pray"; or

"Let us speak to Jesus"; or

"Before my little prayers are said,
I'll fold my hands and bow my head;
I'll try to think to whom I pray
And try to mean the words I say."

SUGGESTED PRAYERS

Come, Lord Jesus, be our Guest,
And let Thy gifts to us be blest. Amen.

Thank You for the world so sweet;
Thank You for the food we eat;
Thank You for the birds that sing —
Thank You, God, for everything.

Heavenly Father, bless this food
To Thy glory and our good. Amen.

Our hands we fold,
Our heads we bow;
For food and drink
We thank Thee now. Amen.

A REST PERIOD IS BENEFICIAL

Time to rest, children dear,
God loves you, and God is near.
Sweetly rest, and do not fear;
God loves you, and He is here.

A period of rest follows most naturally after lunchtime. Before the children ate, they washed their hands and calmed down considerably. After their lunch period they are in a receptive mood for further relaxation.

There is no single good way in which rest periods should be conducted in the kindergarten. The procedure may vary depending on the individual setup.

If the kindergarten meets in an all-day session or for more than two hours, it is advisable to have a scheduled rest time. This rest period is, of course, in addition to the many short and natural breaks that enter into the school day. The length of the period will be determined by the type of rest and by the facilities for a rest.

REST EQUIPMENT

The ideal arrangement would be to have the children rest on small, low cots of canvas, but space and cost of equipment often prohibit this, so a clean rug or bath mat becomes an excellent substitute. Each mother provides a rug for her child on which she sews the child's name. All names should be at the top of the rug on a tape or colored ribbon. The children are taught to fold their rugs so that the inside will always be kept clean. After the rest period each child packs his or her rug neatly away on a shelf or in a locker.

INTRODUCING THE REST PERIOD

Do not attempt a lying-down rest period the first few days of kindergarten, since the children who resent naps at home may react the same way at school. It is better to introduce the period after the children are acquainted with one another and are used to the teacher and her guidance. Other forms of relaxation can take the place of the lying-down rest period for the first—finger plays, games, or resting the head on the table.

When introducing the rest period to the children, it is well to talk it over with them, so they will accept it as a matter of routine. The rest period will then gradually be accepted by the children as a natural part of their kindergarten day.

REST POSITIONS

The teacher will help the children relax in a natural and comfortable position. Some may rest better on their stomachs, others on their sides, and a few on their backs. They should be encouraged to rest just as they do at home. The children must feel free to move or twist if necessary, but no deliberate poking, kicking, or disturbing should be permitted. It is not necessary that the children close their eyes to rest. In fact some may relax better if they are able to see someone else or receive a friendly smile from a friend or from the teacher.

Seldom does a child fall asleep. However, should one do so, it would be advisable to awaken him when the period of rest is over lest he be embarrassed on awaking when he finds the children working on some other activity.

THE TEACHER
DURING THE REST PERIOD

The teacher can do much to create an atmosphere conducive to rest. She should not busy herself with desk duties while the children rest. She is part of the rest period. She may sit quietly at her table and observe the children, speak a soft word or two to the children who may be tense, play a record, play a song softly on the piano, or just be near to lend a feeling of well-being and security.

PART THREE

PROGRAMS AND MATERIALS

13. Planning and Scheduling

A day for little ones should be
Planned with care and orderly,
And filled with all the many joys
That make them happy girls and boys.

PLANNING

The preschool children of today are living in a culture far different than their counterparts of even a dozen years ago. By the time the fours and fives come to school, they have been influenced by radio, television, movies, comic books, all the media a modern culture has to offer. It is quite natural, then, that today's programs of study would differ from those of yesterday.

The basic kindergarten philosophies were an outgrowth of a few brave pioneers in preschool education. These philosophies have remained rather constant except for a few minor changes. The belief that all children should be given the best educational opportunities in harmony with each ones potential still stands, and on this we build.

Research has proven that young children are able to absorb more intellectual content than the conventional kindergarten programs have expected of them. Pushing the first-grade curriculum down into the kindergarten is not the answer for a content-oriented program of study. The answer can best be found in setting up a stimulating, thought-provoking program in an environment where children may build correct concepts, absorb and express ideas, interpret data, and react to the stimuli of learning with confidence and wonder.

A good program will—

1. Provide many opportunities for social growth and intellectual learnings under Christian influences.

2. Provide an environment in which a child may grow physically well and emotionally secure.

3. Provide opportunities for children to work in large learning groups as well as in small interest groups.

4. Plan a program built on the needs and interests of the children involved.

5. Balance the developmental, the creative, and the cognitive learning values.

PROGRAMS ARE DIFFERENT

Since programs of study will be built around the needs of a particular group, in a particular place, and at a particular age level, they will differ from one another.

Let these few statements guide you in planning and proposing:

1. Children live in a totally different world today.

2. Questions are being raised as to the adequacy of the "child development" point of view.

3. Much more is known today about the impact of early intellectual development and its effect on the future learning of the young child.

4. Children have ideas, are able to think, and should be given an environment in which thinking and ideas can be developed.

5. A kindergarten curriculum can be content oriented and still a garden in which tender plants grow according to patterns designed for them by their almighty Creator.

SCHEDULING

The following outline is built around large time blocks of learning and should lend itself to a variety of needs. It should also aid the teacher in maintaining an orderly sequence and in projecting a plan of action. At the same time it allows for flexibility, so necessary in a kindergarten day.

Arrival Time

This is an exciting time for the young child. He thrills at the teacher's friendly greeting. Showing and Sharing at this time is a spontaneous activity much preferred to the stereotyped Show and Tell. This is also a time for free activities.

Moments with God

This involves growing in the Christian faith and life through worship in songs, prayers, Bible stories, pictures, flannelgraph, dramatics, filmstrips, crafts, and projects.

Large Group Activities

The children work together in the content areas of—

Social Studies —including some geographical, historical, and economical conceptual learnings.

Language Arts —oral and written expression including "chart stories" with the group, prereading and reading activities according to the "pacing rate" of individuals.

Science —experiments, new discoveries, films, trips, walks, and some research into the animal and plant world, sound, and space.

Mathematics —learning to use "math" concepts in all areas as the need arises—discovering and solving problems.

Rest and Relaxation

This includes resting, storytime, snacktime, and playtime.

Activities

The activities that follow will be an outgrowth of the content learnings. They will be expressed through—

Art Work —using the different media in small groups.

Music —quiet listening, perhaps in small groups with earphones, and musical activities with all.

Dramatization —for fun or for performance.

Cleaning Up

Closing Time with the Blessing of God

EVALUATING

As a teacher plans for the coming day, she keeps the needs of each child before her and sets her goals accordingly. As she evaluates the outcomes at the end of the day, she may ask herself the following questions:

1. Did I provide many and varied experiences by which the children could grow in their powers of adjustment and in Christian living?

2. Did I make provision for individual differences?

3. Did I allow for participation in activities that foster physical growth and release tensions?

4. Did I challenge intellectual learning without inhibiting creativity?

5. Did I provide sufficient time and space for the children to work easily and freely?

6. Did I encourage discovery and exploration?

7. Did I maintain an attitude of Christian love and encourage the same in the children?

A HALF DAY
IN A CHRISTIAN KINDERGARTEN [1]

Observation was made the middle of May.

[1] This observation was made in the kindergarten of Saint John Lutheran School, Forest Park, Ill.

Number of children enrolled and present: ten girls, seven boys.

Age range of children: 5 years 6 months to 6 years 3 months.

Occupations of fathers: six tradesmen, five businessmen, two medical doctors, one instructor, one banker, one salesman, and one policeman.

Religious background: thirteen Lutheran, two Protestant, and two no church affiliation.

8:15 — 8:50: Free Play

Since the school doors open at 8:15, one or two pupils come with older brothers and sisters and arrive at this time. Susan Jo is one of the early comers. She gives her teacher a friendly greeting and is especially excited today because her mother had a baby girl early this morning. She says the baby's name is Allyson Lynn, and she and her teacher talk about this special event. Since Susan Jo invariably draws a picture when she comes, her teacher suggests that perhaps her mother would like a card. Susan Jo responds enthusiastically and immediately gets the paper and crayons, sits at a table, and makes her card.

Jennie is another early comer. She comes into the room in a businesslike manner and exchanges greetings with the teacher. Susan Jo tells her about the new baby sister. A little chatting takes place between the two girls, but Susan wants to finish the card.

Jennie goes to the chalkboard and writes some words and draws a picture of some people, flowers, sun, and a house. She draws a line around her pictures and writes her name above it to let everyone know that this is her picture and no one should erase it.

By now the first bus has arrived, and a group of children come into the room. It seems everyone has something important to tell. The teacher greets them with, "Good morning, boys and girls."

Jane comes into the room quite excited

because her big brother is going to California on a vacation; she and mother are going to Aunt Clara's for lunch; she's wearing a new dress Aunt Clara made. Some children are crowding around. They have important things to tell too. The teacher suggests to Jane that she save the rest of her news for "Talking Time." Jane accepts this and bounces off with her girlfriend to put a puzzle together.

Kelly comes with a note that she is *not* to take the bus home; mother and Kevin, her brother, are picking her up. Denise brings an envelope containing her milk money. She carefully places it on the teacher's desk. She greets her teacher, engages in a few words of conversation, and decides to play with the mailbox.

Excitement begins anew with the arrival of the second bus. The teacher and pupils exchange greetings. Joel puts a small paper bag on the teacher's desk and says, "Open it, it's yours." Mother baked a cake, and Joel and John, twins, brought a piece for teacher. John hasn't said anything; he smiles and lets his brother do all the talking. The teacher gives both Joel and John a little hug and says she'll eat the cake when she has her lunch.

Tommy, Kim, and Sally have decided to play "dress up" and are pretending they are a mother, a grandmother, and a lady who takes care of dogs. Each is wearing a long dress and jewelry. The lady who takes care of dogs is carrying a stuffed dog.

Daryl, Brian, and Doris decide to do some finger painting and become fascinated with mixing colors and the designs their fingers make.

Robbie, who came just as it was time to put away the toys, stops at the fishbowl to watch the guppies. He places the large magnifying glass against the fishbowl to see better and remarks that he just saw the snail stick out its head.

The teacher plays several chords on the piano, indicating that things must be put away. Several children moan a bit, but they accept the fact that playtime is over. Each child sits down at a table and puts his head down as the lights are turned out. While the children rest, the teacher checks attendance. One child quietly walks to the washroom off the classroom.

8:50 – 9:15: Sharing Experiences

After several minutes of quiet, the lights are turned on and the teacher sings the "Good Morning" song, and the pupils sing their reply. Doris says her family is going to Germany for five weeks, but Father can't go because he gets only three weeks vacation. Sally is wearing a new dress. Bobby brings a bag and wants his teacher to open it—in it are two lovely peonies that Mommy picked.

After they are all "talked out," the group pledges allegiance to the flag. They settle down near the chalkboard and discuss the day, the numeral for the day, the name of the month, and the year. A child marks the calendar, and the teacher begins writing "Our Newspaper." The writing of a newspaper has developed from the early part of kindergarten, when the date was written, and by now has developed into this:

Our Newspaper

Today is Tuesday, May 27, 1975.
It is a sunny, warm day.
17 boys and girls are here.
No one is absent.
Danny is our "Cookie Boy."

The class plays a game with the story—drawing lines around words beginning with certain letters, around numerals, names of children, the month, etc.

The teacher says, "Now let's get all the wiggles out and say:

I wiggle my fingers.
I wiggle my toes.
I wiggle my body.
I wiggle my nose.
Now, all my wiggles are gone out of me,
And I'll be as quiet as I can be."

Children and teacher do the actions as they say the rhyme.

9:15 — 9:45: Jesus Time

The children suggest their favorite Jesus songs: "I Am Jesus' Little Lamb" and "Jesus Is My Shepherd."

After singing, the children and teacher talk about being Jesus' lamb and how much Jesus loves them. This leads to the question of when they really became Jesus' child. Susan Anne says she became Jesus' child through Baptism. Brian says he became Jesus' child when he heard about Jesus in Sunday school and in kindergarten.

"Today, boys and girls, I'm going to tell you the true story about a man who hated Jesus. He hated Him so much that he killed the Christians, the people who believed in Jesus. Let's hear this story." Having made sure each child is seated comfortably, the teacher begins to tell the story of Saul who hated the people who believed in Jesus.

One day a man by the name of Saul heard there were some Christians in the city of Damascus, so he said, "I must go over there and kill those Christians." As Saul and some of his friends walked along the road to Damascus, a bright light came on Saul. He got so scared he fell to the ground. With the bright light was a voice, which said, "Saul, Saul, why are you hurting Me?" Saul shook all over and said, "Who are you?" And the voice said, "I am Jesus, whom you're hurting." Saul, still lying on the ground, said, "What do You want me to do?" And the Voice, Jesus, said, "Go into the city; there you will meet a man who will tell you what to do."

The great light was gone. Saul got up from the ground, but he couldn't see anything. He was blind, and his friends had to help him find his way into the city. As they came into the city, a man named Ananias met them and said, "Come to my house and stay with me and my family." Ananias was a Christian, and somehow Jesus had told Ananias to meet Saul and his friends.

Saul and his friends stayed with Ananias and his family for three days. During that time Ananias talked to Saul and his friends about Jesus and His love for His people. Hearing this good news moved Saul so much that he said, "I'm sorry for having been such a bad guy. I want to be Jesus' child. I want to hear more about this Jesus. Baptize me." So Ananias baptized Saul, and his name was changed to Paul. All at once Paul's eyes could see again. His blindness was gone!

Paul and his friends left Ananias' house, and Paul was a different person. He talked to people about Jesus and His great love. Paul went into faraway cities and countries and told the people about Jesus. Sometimes people were mean to Paul because he talked about Jesus. They'd put Paul in jail, throw stones at him, or whip him, but Paul never stopped. He kept going from place to place telling people about Jesus. Paul was one of the greatest missionaries Jesus ever had.

The teacher and pupils discuss the story. The teacher asks, "If we are Jesus' children, what's our job?" One child raises his hand and says, "Show our love to Jesus." Robbie says, "I show my love to Jesus when I don't hit my sister." The Jesus Time is closed with several ex corde prayers by the teacher and children. Kim prays, "Dear Jesus, help me grow in showing my love to You. Amen." The teacher closes with a prayer, "Dear Jesus, we do wrong things and sin, but we're sorry. Please help us grow in showing our love to You. Help us today when we play and work here in kindergarten. We know You love us; help us show our love to You. Amen."

9:45 — 10:05: Physical Activities

The children run, skip, gallop, or relax according to the recorded music or as the teacher plays the piano. Some exercises are done to a "physical fitness" record — bending, jumping, swinging arms, and running in place. The activities are concluded with a game, "Go Round the Village."

10:05 – 10:40: Washroom – Snack – Rest

The children line up by the door and quietly walk to the washroom. After washroom duties are finished, the children walk to the refrigerator, get their milk, and walk back to their room. The "cookie boy" is ready to pass out his cookies. When everyone is ready, each bows his head, folds his hands, and prays,

> "Our hands we fold;
> Our heads we bow,
> For food and drink we thank
> Thee now. Amen."

Cookies are passed out, and Susan Anne asks, "Are there nuts in these cookies?" Danny replies, "Yes." Susan Anne says, "No, thank you, I can't eat nuts." Conversation gets a little excited at times. Tammy took her straw out of the carton and dripped milk on the floor, so she wipes it up. Robbie has a joke to tell: "What's yellow and flies?" After a few wild guesses, Robbie says, "A super banana." When everyone has finished, the children return thanks.

The children get their rugs and mats in an orderly fashion, the teacher draws the drapes, and the lights are turned out. As the children lie on their rugs, the phonograph is playing the "Sleepy Forest." A "wake-up brownie" is chosen to touch each child, thus notifying him that resting time is over.

10:40 – 11:00: Together Time

The children sit in a circle on the floor and the *Weekly Reader Surprise* is passed out. Today they "read" pages 2 and 3. The teacher asks questions about page 3, which shows a goose covered with oil swimming in dirty, oily water. Frank says he sees a goose, only it looks funny—all oily, and its feathers are dirty. Someone says maybe a big ship put the oil in the water. Then they look at page 3 where a man is putting straw in the water, and they all wonder why.

The teacher performs a little experiment to show them "why." She takes a pan and fills it with clean water. Then she squirts oil onto the water. The children put their fingers into the oily water. Sally says, "Ugh! That's greasy water; I don't like that." Several children make similar comments. Now the teacher takes some of the paper towels with which the children wiped their hands and places them into the oily water. One child says, "Look, all the grease is going into the paper towel." After they notice the removal of oil from the water with the paper towels, the teacher directs the class's attention to page 3. Mike says, "I bet that straw soaks up the oil." The discussion concludes with the thought that the man is cleaning the lake.

Bobby raises his hand and wants to read what it says. He reads, "Our Big World; Water Pollution." Then discussion follows about the time several couldn't go swimming because the lake was so dirty, even had garbage in it. The class talks about what can be done to keep lakes and rivers clean. Several point out that bottles and paper shouldn't be thrown into water. They decide not to be "litterbugs." The teacher asks about the schoolyard, and the children decide to pick up paper from the yard.

11:00 – 11:20: Outdoor Activities

As the children prepare to go outdoors to pick up paper, the teacher says she has a large paper bag to put the "litter" in. The children are excited about the project and do a good job of cleaning up. Following this the teacher suggests they play "Duck, Duck, Goose." After everyone has had his turn, they play on the monkey bars.

11:20 – 11:30: Closing Activities

The children line up at the entrance. When all "outside noises" are ready to stay outside, they quietly walk into the classroom. They are ready for a short story that one of the children brought. After reading the story, the teacher asks them to stand, since it's time to go home.

She suggests that they stand in a prayer circle and think of something special they want to tell Jesus. Doris prays, "Thank You, Jesus, for loving me. Help me not to hit my brother. Amen." Laura prays, "Thank You for my mommy, daddy, and teachers. Amen." They sing "The Day Is Done."

The bus children line up by the door. The patrol boy will lead them to the bus. The teacher says, "Good-bye, boys and girls. Remember who you are." Brian smiles a big grin and says, "I'm Jesus' child." The teacher says, "See you all tomorrow." The children are dismissed in an orderly manner.

14. Equipment and Supplies

Adequate facilities and good equipment help provide rich experiences, but they are not ends in themselves.

EQUIPMENT SHOULD SERVE THE NEEDS

No one person can determine what equipment is needed in every kindergarten. This will be decided by the needs of the group, the aims of the kindergarten, and the budget designated for this purpose.

The equipment and supplies should, however, add to the development of a functional program. Poor equipment may not add to a challenging learning environment and may even curtail the effectiveness of an otherwise well-planned program.

Even little children can appreciate a well-equipped room where they can play and work with things that are made for their use, things that fit their size.

There is no such thing as equipment for its own sake. It must serve the needs of the pupils in the kindergarten. Anything that does not serve their needs is superfluous and need not occupy space in the room.

It is hoped that the following suggestions will give the creative teacher impetus to expand, add, and invent new ideas.

FURNITURE

Since the schedule of the kindergarten is to be functional and flexible, the furniture arrangement must be likewise. It should be movable so that it can be easily arranged for the various activities and grouped according to the needs that may arise.

Small tables and chairs provide adequate working space for the children. (Suggested sizes: top—18"×36", 20"×40", or 24"×36", and 20"—24" high.)

The chairs should be chosen so that the top of the table is about 10 inches above the seat of the chair.

The tables may be made of old lumber and covered with Formica, which makes a very fine and durable tabletop. The children can use them freely and wash them off by themselves after painting and clay work. Firm, nicely painted benches make good substitutes for chairs around the worktables. The children like to use them, for they can easily change from a sitting to a kneeling position.

A round or oblong table for library books, or for a corner of interest, with several chairs grouped around it, comes in handy when additional table space is needed.

FLOOR COVERINGS

An 8'×10' or 9'×12' rug in a corner of the room makes the room cozy and warm and is an ideal place for conversation time, storytime, and quiet games. It may also be used for the rest period if the children do not have individual rugs on which to lie.

If the floor is not covered with lino-tile or linoleum, it is advisable to buy a small congoleum rug with a nursery rhyme design and place it on the floor where the children may paint or paste. This rug can be easily washed up each day and kept clean for the children to sit and play. Indoor-outdoor carpeting is also well suited for a floor covering.

STORAGE SPACE

Shelves that are to be used by the children should be low, deep, and wide, so that they can easily hold their toys, large drawings, and supplies. Shelving is most useful if made with compartments of various dimensions both vertically and horizontally. Horizontal divisions can be so arranged as to provide mostly 12-inch divisions with some 6- and 24-inch sections. The vertical compartment subdivided at 6, 12, 24, and 36 inches will provide compartments of sufficient variation to accommodate the many things that are used daily. Shelves should not be more than 42 inches from the floor.

Besides open shelves for the children's supplies, there should be ample space for storage. Many things will not be used frequently and will have to be kept in a closed place in the meantime. The teacher will also want plenty of space in which to keep paper, paints, and other necessary supplies. If cupboards cannot be built into the room, a small room nearby will serve the purpose.

In addition to cupboard and locker space, it is good to have a chest or large wooden box (2'×2'×4') in which materials can be stored. If this is on wheels or casters, it is easily moved.

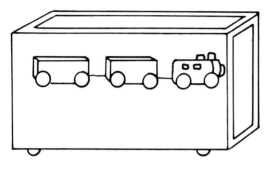

Woodbox for Toys

A drag-box, in which blocks may be kept, is an aid to keeping things in order and accessible to the children.

OTHER EQUIPMENT

Flannelgraph. A flannelgraph board, preferably one that can be folded and stored away when not in use, is a great help in telling stories and illustrating experiences.

Easels. Every kindergarten room should have several low easels, at which the children can paint and draw freely. These should stand near the door or near the sink so that the children can get to the water easily.

Easels can be bought or constructed out of scrap lumber. Large boards can also be placed on the chalkboard ledge and used by the children as easels.

Easels may be constructed by using four 54″ standards made of 1″×2″ lumber. These are hinged or bolted at the top. A sheet of plywood 30″×26″ is fastened to each side. A detachable trough for holding paint jars should be attached below the board, and clips at the top.

Chalkboard. A chalkboard, 20″−22″ from the floor, affords the children many happy hours of experimentation and creation. It should be available at all times to the children, and they should be encouraged to use it freely for fun.

Bulletin Boards. Bulletin boards, made of wallboard or cork, afford the children great pleasure. They, too, should be low enough to allow the children to pin up their own drawings and to decorate their own room. They will enjoy bringing news items and things of interest to school, if they are allowed to post them on the bulletin board themselves.

Musical Instruments. A good record player is a necessity. It will find daily use in a kindergarten. A piano is also very desirable. The piano need not be beautiful, but it must be in tune.

Easel

Dollhouse. A dollhouse with all the accessories—dishes, dolls, broom, mops, buggies, telephones, stoves, doll clothes, and clothespins—should be given a corner in the room. An aquarium, a terrarium, a birdcage, garden tools, wagons, and a tricycle, if possible, should be available for use when the occasion demands it.

Cutting Instruments. A paper cutter and a scissors rack, where children may place their scissors when not in use, add to the efficiency and orderliness of the kindergarten program.

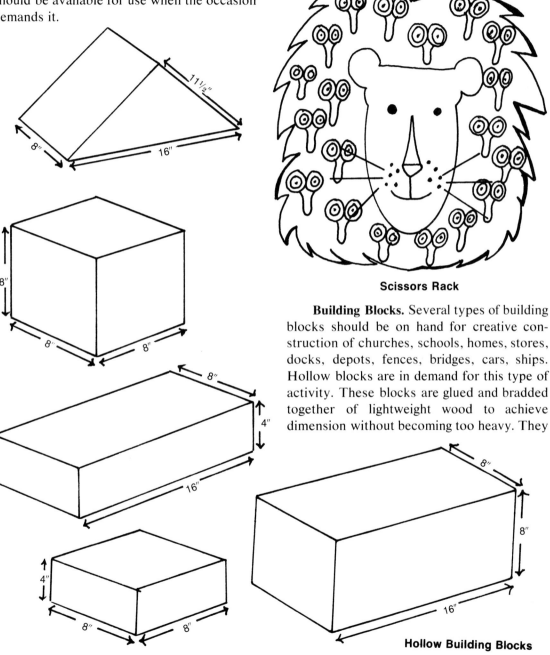

Scissors Rack

Building Blocks. Several types of building blocks should be on hand for creative construction of churches, schools, homes, stores, docks, depots, fences, bridges, cars, ships. Hollow blocks are in demand for this type of activity. These blocks are glued and bradded together of lightweight wood to achieve dimension without becoming too heavy. They

Hollow Building Blocks

167

can be bought or may be constructed in the following dimensions: 4″×8″×8″, 8″×8″×8″, 16″×8″×8″, and 16″×8″×4″. To the blocks should be added 8″ boards, 32″ and 48″ long, and 4″ boards, 16″ and 32″ in length. Cylinders, half cylinders, triangles, and arches of corresponding dimensions may be added. A set of 20 of each of the first two sizes and 10 of each of the next two sizes of blocks, plus 12 of each of the boards, will make a good combination. Six triangles with a 16″×8″ base will permit a variety of construction.

Solid blocks are very useful. These are obtainable or can be made of 1″ material, 3″ wide and in lengths of 6″, 12″, and 24″. This set too can be expanded with half-width or with double-thickness units and with cylinders, triangles, and arches. This type is particularly suitable for layout work on the floor to represent walks, railroad tracks, fences, or merely the floor plan for various buildings and furnishings.

Sets of toy blocks may be added, but these do not compare in functional value with the types described above.

Worship Aids. Worship may become a little more meaningful to the children if a small, simply constructed altar is used. This could provide the setting for the worship service. On or near the altar should be a large Bible with pictures, a cross, several Bible story books, and perhaps some candles or a vase of flowers.

Other materials used in the religious hour include:

The Concordia Teaching Pictures
The flannelgraph
Bible story recordings
Puzzles of religious subjects
Pictures
A manger scene
Illustrated prayer books
Filmstrips

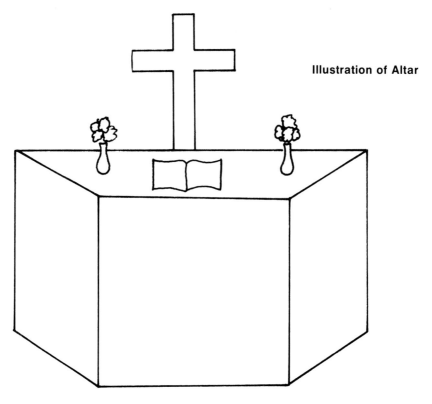

Illustration of Altar

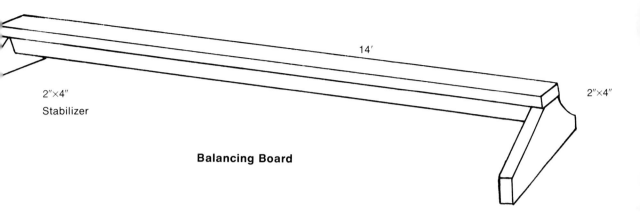

14'

2"×4"
Stabilizer

Balancing Board

2"×4"

MAKING THE LEARNING REAL

When activities are organized around life situations, materials should be provided to make these situations as real as possible. When the children participate in their language activities and in their social studies, the teaching will be more effective if they can dramatize and actually live these life situations with equipment that approximates reality.

Observing the hand of the Creator suggests an aquarium and a terrarium for animal and plant life, a flower garden or seed box, a fishbowl or turtle bowl, a cage for pets that may be brought to school, magnets, and magnifying glasses.

Work in the home suggests small furniture, cooking and eating dishes, a broom, dust mop, and dustpan.

Community helpers suggest trucks, wagons, buses, cars, fire engines, milk carts, a post office.

Farm life suggests animals, a barn, a truck, a tractor, and garden tools.

Social living among the children during the day is aided by toy telephones, puzzles, blocks, picture books, pegboards, beanbags, balls, jump ropes, dolls, doll buggies, a watering can, rhythm instruments, wheelbarrows, jeeps, airplanes, and any toys that children at this age enjoy. Multimedia materials offer many opportunities to make learning real.

PLAY EQUIPMENT

Materials for play activities are infinite. For outdoor use things should be chosen that bring exercise to the muscles not used too frequently indoors. A long log, slightly sunken in the ground, is excellent for the child to learn balance. A balancing board, consisting of a sturdy board fastened 8 to 12 inches above the ground, will also challenge the child to maintain his balance while walking across it.

Children enjoy bars, the slide, and the small jungle gym. A climbing rope can be quite challenging too. This should be a heavy-gauge hemp rope, safely suspended from the ceiling or sturdy tree and weighted down at the bottom to prevent swaying. Knots may be tied in the rope for grips. Horizontal bars may be fastened securely in between a doorway. Fixtures may be placed so that the bars may be put in at different heights.

EQUIPMENT FOR ART
AND CONSTRUCTIVE ACTIVITIES

To carry on some of the art and constructive activities, tools and art supplies are needed. Some of the most necessary supplies are:

Paintbrushes—for the easel and for individual use.

Paints—cold-water paint (powder paint) in various colors; some ordinary house paint; a few cans of enamel.

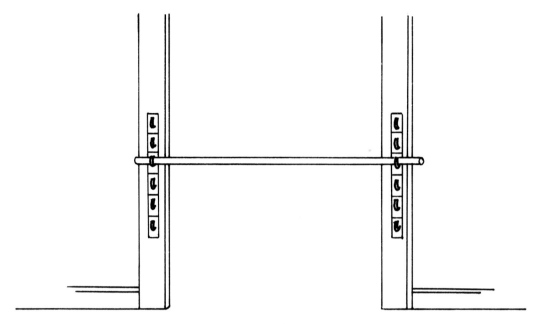

Horizontal Bar

Crayons — all colors in the large jumbo size.

Charcoal.

Newsprint — for drawing and painting.

Manila paper — 18″×24″, also 12″×18″.

Construction paper — in various colors.

Brown wrapping paper — in a roll for drawing of scenes and friezes.

Tagboard — for signs and charts.

Shelf paper — for finger painting.

Clay — powder for modeling.

Paste.

Cotton batting — for stuffing.

Old wallpaper books — for trimming.

Boxes — all sorts and shapes.

Paper fasteners.

Paper napkins.

Paper plates.

Empty spools.

Straws.

THE TEACHER MUST SURVEY HER NEEDS

Whereas none of the things that have been suggested are absolutely essential to the growth and well-being of a kindergarten child, they are worthwhile and could be used to advantage in the kindergarten program. The suggestions are intended merely to serve as guidelines — a beginning on which to build.

It will be necessary for each kindergarten teacher to survey her particular field, study her particular children, set up a budget that will meet the approval of her congregation, and then choose those things that will give the children the maximum growth and development. Items of permanent equipment can be added from year to year. It is surprising what can be acquired in the course of a few years through careful planning.

See also Bibliography.

BIBLIOGRAPHY

I. EARLY EDUCATION AND THE GROWING CHILD

Anderson, R. H., and H. G. Shane, eds. *As the Twig Is Bent: Readings in Early Childhood Education.* Boston: Houghton Mifflin Co., 1971.

Association for Childhood Education International. *Early Childhood Crucial Years for Learning.* Washington, D. C., 1966.

 This compilation of 22 articles from the periodical *Childhood Education* is a valuable addition to the teacher's library as a basic resource of thought concerning early childhood education before 1966. The articles are nontechnical, written for teachers, and interesting.

Gray, Susan W., et al. *Before First Grade: Training Project for Culturally Disadvantaged Children.* New York: Teachers College Press, Columbia University, 1966.

 An overview of the curriculum developed for 4- and 5-year-old culturally deprived children. Detailing of specific objectives for educational programs for disadvantaged children includes descriptions of specific classroom activities.

Headley, Neith E., *Education in the Kindergarten.* New York: Van Nostrand-Reinhold, 1966.

 A basic text in kindergarten education. Offers helpful resource suggestions for the curriculum.

Hechinger, Fred M., ed. *Pre-School Education Today.* New York: Doubleday & Co., 1966.

 A compilation of writings illustrating major innovations in curriculum development for young children. Technical reading.

Heffernan, Helen, and V. E. Todd. *The Years Before School.* New York: The Macmillan Co., 1964.

 A comprehensive text for use by teachers, parents, administrators, and all who deal with the education of the preschool child. Contains suggestions for adult groups interested in arranging for preschool groups and a detailed description of the curriculum for the 3- and 4-year-old in school. Especially recommended for groups considering the organization of an educational program for young children.

Hymes, James L. *Early Childhood Education.* Washington, D. C.: National Association for the Education of Young Children, 1968.

Jenkins, William A., et al. *These Are Your Children.* Glenview, Ill.: Scott, Foresman & Co., 1966.

 Description of the various age levels and general characteristics of each. Practical and useful.

Kagan, J. *Understanding Children.* New York: Harcourt Brace Jovanovich, Inc., 1971.

Landreth, Catherine. *Early Childhood: Behavior and Learning.* New York: Alfred A. Knopf, 1967.

 A valuable resource that evaluates the research and the applications of psychology in the areas of early childhood. Teachers will find intensive discussions in the areas of behavior and learning patterns of children. Somewhat technical reading.

Leeper, Sarah, et al. *Good Schools for Young Children.* New York: The Macmillan Co., 1968.

 Included in the first section (a discussion of rationale for early childhood education) are descriptions of the many types of programs now existing and an overview of recent research in the field. Teachers and administrators will find the sections concerning curricular matters and organization of programs helpful. Easy reading. References at the end of each chapter.

Logan, Lillian M. *Teaching the Young Child.* Boston: Houghton Mifflin Co., 1960.

 Still one of the finest discussions of methods for use with young children. Written first for student teachers, even the most experienced will find many practical ideas for revitalizing and improving teaching practices.

Morrison, Ida E., and Ida Perry. *Kindergarten-Primary Education: Teaching Procedures.* New York: Ronald Press Co., 1961.

 A basic book for the teacher of young children. Originally written for teacher trainees, the book presents extensive coverage of the various subjects in the curriculum, with special emphasis on reading and language training.

Robinson, Helen, and Bernard Spodek. *New Directions in the Kindergarten.* New York: Teachers College Press, Columbia University, 1967.

The major challenge to kindergarten curriculum today is *content.* From this premise the authors present a practical discussion and application of the intellectual phase of curriculum for young children. The authors outline major topics for development within the curriculum and illustrate their development in the classroom. Major disciplines such as economics, anthropology, history, and geography are included in the curriculum for young children. A challenging yet practical publication for early childhood educators. This is the first in a series of publications: Early Childhood Education Series, Kenneth D. Wann, editor.

Other books in the series include:

Gray and Klaus. *Before First Grade,* 1966.

Taylor, Katharine. *Parents and Children Learn Together,* 1968.

Hamlin et al. *Schools for Young Disadvantaged Children,* 1968.

Wann, Kenneth, et al. *Fostering Intellectual Development in Young Children.* New York: Teachers College Press, Columbia University, 1965.

This is the report of a study by the authors that gives evidence of greater intellectual abilities among 3- to 5-year-olds than is often supposed. The authors suggest basic strategies for an educational program that guides and supports intellectual development of young children. The nontechnical approach of the book makes it inviting reading.

Ward, Evangeline H. *Early Childhood Education.* Dansville, New York: F. A. Owen Publishing Co., 1968.

A useful discussion of a traditional-type educational setting for ages 3 – 5. Contains ten pages of lists for materials and equipment to be used in the classroom interest centers. Description of learning centers in classroom is especially well done.

II. EARLY EDUCATION AND THE CHANGING CURRICULUM

Burgess, Evangeline. *Values in Early Childhood Education.* Department of Elementary-Kindergarten-Nursery Education. Washington, D. C.: National Education Association, 1965.

Croft and Hess. *An Activities Handbook for Teachers of Young Children.* Boston: Houghton Mifflin Co., 1971.

Durkin, Dolores. *Children Who Read Early.* New York: Teachers College Press, Columbia University, 1966.

Fleming, Robert. *Curriculum for Today's Boys and Girls.* Columbus, Ohio: Chas. E. Merrill Publishing Co., 1966.

Ginsberg, Herbert, and Sylvia Opper, eds. *Piaget's Theory of Intellectual Development: An Introduction.* Englewood Cliffs, N. J.: Prentice-Hall, 1969.

Goodlad, John I., et al. *The Changing School Curriculum.* New York: Fund for the Advancement of Education, 1966.

Gould, Josephine T. *Growing with Nursery and Kindergarten Children.* Boston: Beacon Press, 1966.

Graham, Winona. *Toward Better Kindergartens.* Washington, D. C.: Association for Childhood Education International, 1966.

Hymes, James. *Teaching the Child Under Six.* Columbus, Ohio: Chas. E. Merrill Publishing Co., 1968.

Ilg, Frances L., and Louise B. Ames. *School Readiness.* New York: Harper & Row, Publishers, 1965.

Pines, Maya. *Revolution in Learning: The Years from Birth to Six.* New York: Harper & Row, Publishers, 1967.

Pitcher, Evelyn, et al. *Helping Young Children Learn.* Columbus, Ohio: Chas. E. Merrill Publishing Co., 1966.

Schmidt, Velma. *A Study of the Influence of Certain Preschool Educational Movements on Contemporary Preschool Practices.* Unpublished Doctoral Dissertation, Lincoln, Nebr.: University of Nebraska, 1968.

Williams, L. *Independent Learning.* Washington, D. C.: American Association of Elementary-Kindergarten-Nursery Educators, 1969.

Wills, Clarice, and Lucille Lindberg. *Kindergarten for Today's Children.* Chicago: Follett Publishing Co., 1967.

III. EARLY EDUCATION AND THE SPECIAL AREAS

Bereiter, Carl, and Siegfried Englemann. *Teaching Disadvantaged Children in the Preschool.* Englewood Cliffs, N. J.: Prentice-Hall, 1966.

172

Bloom, Benjamin, et al. *Compensatory Education for Cultural Deprivation.* New York: Holt, Rinehart & Winston, 1965.

Montessori in Perspective. Washington, D. C.: National Association for the Education of Young Children, 1966.

Passow, A. Harry, et al. *Education of the Disadvantaged.* New York: Holt, Rinehart & Winston, Inc., 1967.

Read, Katherine. *The Nursery School.* Philadelphia: W. B. Saunders Co., 1966.

Schloss, Samuel. *Enrollment of 3-, 4-, and 5-year Olds in Nursery Schools and Kindergartens.* Washington, D. C.: U. S. Department of Health, Education, and Welfare, 1965.

Schramm, Wilbur, et al. *Television in the Lives of Our Children.* Stanford, Calif.: Stanford University Press, 1961.

IV. EARLY EDUCATION
AND THE LANGUAGE LEARNINGS

Arbuthnot, May. *Children and Books.* Glenview, Ill.: Scott, Foresman & Co., 1964.

Barbe, Walter. *Creative Writing Activities.* Columbus, Ohio: Highlights for Children, 1967.

Betty, Walter, and Mary Bowen. *Slithery Snakes and Other Aids to Children's Writing.* New York: Appleton-Century-Crofts, 1967.

Chall, Jeanne. *Learning to Read: The Great Debate.* New York: McGraw-Hill Book Co., 1967.

Fitzgerald, Burdette S. *World Tales for Creative Dramatics and Story-telling.* Englewood Cliffs, N. J.: Prentice-Hall, 1962.

Herrick, V. E., and Marcella Nerbovig. *Using Experience Charts with Children.* Columbus, Ohio: Chas. E. Merrill Books, 1964.

Hollowell, Lillian, ed. *A Book of Children's Literature.* New York: Holt, Rinehart & Winston, 1966.

Howard, Vernon. *Puppet & Pantomime Plays.* New York: Sterling Publishing Co., 1962.

Huck, Charlotte, and Doris Young Kuhn. *Children's Literature in the Elementary School.* New York: Holt, Rinehart & Winston, 1968.

Lamb, Rose. *Guiding Children's Language Learning.* Dubuque, Iowa: William C. Brown Co., 1969.

Lee, Dorris, and Richard Allen. *Learning to Read Through Experience.* New York: Appleton-Century-Crofts, 1963.

Nohl, Frederick, and Frederick Meyer, eds. *A Curriculum Guide for Lutheran Elementary Schools.* Vol. I. St. Louis: Concordia Publishing House, 1964.

Rasmussen, Carrie. *Let's Say Poetry Together and Have Fun.* 2 Vols. (Vol. 1, grades 1–3). Minneapolis: Burgess Publishing Co., 1962.

Shane, Harold G. *Linguistics and the Classroom Teacher.* Washington, D. C.: Association for Supervision and Curriculum Development, 1967.

Taylor, Loren E. *Puppetry, Marionettes and Shadow Plays.* Minneapolis: Burgess Publishing Co., 1965.

Walker, Pamela. *Seven Steps to Creative Children's Dramatics.* New York: Hill & Wang, 1957.

Ward, Winifred. *Playmaking with Children, from Kindergarten Through Junior High School.* New York: Appleton-Century-Crofts, 1959.

V. EARLY EDUCATION AND THE SOCIAL STUDIES

Calderone, M. S. "Sex Education and the Very Young Child," *PTA Magazine,* 61:2 (1966), 16–18.

Dunfee, Maxine, and Helen Sagl. *Social Studies Through Problem Solving.* New York: Holt, Rinehart & Winston, 1966.

Frey, M. K. *I Wonder, I Wonder* (Concordia Sex Education Series, for ages 5 to 8). St. Louis: Concordia Publishing House, 1967.

Jarolimek, John. *Social Studies in Elementary Education.* New York: The Macmillan Co., 1967.

Joyce, Bruce R. *Toward Humanity: A Manifesto for the Social Studies.* Washington, D. C.: National Education Association, Center for the Study of Instruction, 1970.

– – –. *Teacher & His Staff: Men, Media, & Machines.* Washington, D. C.: National Education Association, Center for the Study of Instruction, 1967.

Nohl, Frederick, and Frederick Meyer, eds. *A Curricu-*

lum Guide for Lutheran Elementary Schools. Vol. I. St. Louis: Concordia Publishing House, 1964.

Torrance, E. Paul. *Creativity.* No. 18 of What Research Says to the Teacher Series. Washington, D. C.: National Education Association, 1964.

VI. EARLY EDUCATION AND RELIGION

A Curriculum Guide. Detroit Board of Christian Education, The Lutheran Church—Missouri Synod, 16257 Nine Mile Road, Detroit, Mich.

Gilbert, W. Kent. *The Age Group Objectives of Christian Education.* The Board of Parish Education of The American Ev. Lutheran Church, The Augustana Lutheran Church, The Suomi Synod, and The United Lutheran Church in America, 1958.

> A detailed outline of growth characteristics of children, ages two through adolescence; basic religious concepts to be developed for each age; suggested activities to develop concepts. Helpful to the development of religious curriculum for young children. A fine addition to the teacher's library.

Griffen, Estelle. *A Core Curriculum for Christian Kindergartens.* Minneapolis: Augsburg Publishing House.

Nohl, Frederick, and Frederick Meyer, eds. *A Curriculum Guide for Lutheran Elementary Schools.* Vol. I. St. Louis: Concordia Publishing House, 1964 (Religion Section Revised 1971).

> This first in a three-volume series is a guide for the primary teacher in the Lutheran school. In addition to brief statements of philosophy, many sample units are outlined for all subject-matter areas in kindergarten through grade three. Religion units are included.

Wangerin, Walter, ed. *Concordia Primary Catechism Readers.* St. Louis: Concordia Publishing House, 1968.

> A series of six religion books for children ages 5—8. Each reader is developed around one of the chief parts of the Catechism and is geared both through vocabulary and presentation to the primary child. A teachers manual accompanies the series and is designed to aid teachers develop a one- to two-week classroom religion unit. The following Primary Readers are included in the series:

> 1. *God Loves You*
> 2. *God Makes Me His Child in Baptism*
> 3. *God Invites Me to Pray*
> 4. *God Gives Me His Law*
> 5. *God Made You Somebody Special*
> 6. *God Comes to Me in Worship*

Early Formal Religious Education

The Mission:Life program or curriculum for formal religious education on preprimary levels offers quarterly Teachers Kits and Pupil Packets containing a great variety of materials in four color-coded programs. A Blue program offers material for five sessions per week and a Red program provides suggestions for two one-hour sessions a week.

A Green program of weekly lessons intended primarily for Sunday morning classes is available on both the Nursery and Kindergarten levels in a two-year parallel sequence, and Orange courses are designed mainly for summer programs.

Each Teachers Kit is built around course units, themes, and session plans presented in a Teachers Guide. A prekindergarten series of three quarterly courses in addition to the kindergarten courses will soon be available also in the Blue and Red programs.

A practical paperback on the teaching of religion to the very young is *The Church Teaching Her Young,* by Allan Hart Jahsmann (St. Louis: Concordia Publishing House, 1967). An instructors guide accompanies the text.

VII. EARLY EDUCATION AND THE AESTHETIC LIFE

Boardman, Eunice, et al. *Exploring Music, Kindergarten.* New York: Holt, Rinehart & Winston, 1969.

Boeve, Edgar. *Children's Art and the Christian Teacher.* St. Louis: Concordia Publishing House, 1966.

Brott, Victor. *Discovering Through Art.* St. Louis: Concordia Publishing House, 1969.

Hildner, V. G., et al. *Joyfully Sing.* St. Louis: Concordia Publishing House, 1961.

McCall, Adeline. *This Is Music for Kindergarten & Nursery School.* Rockleigh, N. J.: Allyn and Bacon, 1965.

Mealy, Norman and Margaret. *Sing for Joy.* New York: Seabury Press, Inc., 1961.

Miller, Elfrieda. *Religious Arts and Crafts for Children.* St. Louis: Concordia Publishing House, 1966.

Nohl, Frederick, and Frederick Meyer, eds. *A Curriculum Guide for Lutheran Elementary Schools.* Vol. I. St. Louis: Concordia Publishing House, 1964.

VIII. EARLY EDUCATION AND ITS APPROACH TO SCIENCE

Beauchamp, Wilbur. *Science Is Fun.* Glenview, Ill.: Scott, Foresman & Co., 1968.

Bernard, J. D. *Science for Tomorrow's World.* New York: The Macmillan Co., 1966.

Blough, Glenn, and Julius Schwartz. *Elementary School Science and How to Teach It.* New York: Holt, Rinehart & Winston, 1964.

Brandwein, Paul, et al. *Concepts in Science Primer.* New York: Harcourt, Brace & World, 1967.

Nohl, Frederick, and Frederick Meyer, eds. *A Curriculum Guide for Lutheran Elementary Schools.* Vol. I. St. Louis: Concordia Publishing House, 1964. (Science Section Revised 1970.)

Renner, John, and William Ragen. *Teaching Science in the Elementary School.* New York: Harper & Row, Publishers, 1968.

Major Elementary Science Curriculum Projects

AAS (Science—A Process Approach)—American Association for the Advancement of Science, 1515 Massachusetts Ave., N.W., Washington, D.C. 20005.

COPES—Conceptually Oriented Program in Elementary Science, Morris H. Shamas, New York University, 4 Washington Place, New York, N.Y. 10003.

ESS—Elementary Science Study, Randolph Brown, Educational Development Center, 55 Chapel St., Newton, Mass. 02160.

ESSP (California)—Elementary School Science Project, Herbert L. Mason, Room 4533, Tolman, University of California, Berkeley, Calif. 94720.

ESSP (Illinois)—J. Myron Atkin and Stanley P. Wyatt, 805 W. Pennsylvania, University of Illinois, Urbana, Ill. 61801.

MinneMAST—Minnesota Mathematics and Science Teaching Project, James Werntz Jr., Minnemath Center, 720 Washington Ave., S.E., Minneapolis, Minn. 55414.

SCIS—Science Curriculum Improvement Study, Robert Karplus, Lawrence Hall of Science, University of California, Berkeley, Calif. 94720.

IX. EARLY EDUCATION AND ITS APPROACH TO MATHEMATICS

Association of Teachers of Mathematics. *Notes on Mathematics in Primary Schools.* New York: Cambridge University Press, 1967.

Buffie, Edward, et al. *Mathematics: Strategies of Teaching.* Englewood Cliffs, N.J.: Prentice-Hall, 1968.

Davis, Robert, ed. *The Changing Curriculum: Mathematics.* Washington, D.C.: Association for Supervision and Curriculum Development, 1967.

Educational Research Council of Greater Cleveland. Key Topics in Math for the Primary Teacher. Chicago: Science Research Associates, 1961.

Garner, M. V. *Mathematics for Elementary School Teachers.* Pacific Palisades, Calif.: Goodyear Publishing Co., 1969.
    This introduces the in-service teacher to mathematics as a logical system—a blend of the modern with the traditional.

Heimer, Ralph, and Miriam Newman. *The New Mathematics for Parents.* New York: Holt, Rinehart & Winston, 1965.

Nohl, Frederick, and Frederick Meyer, eds. *A Curriculum Guide for Lutheran Elementary Schools.* Vol. I. St. Louis: Concordia Publishing House, 1964. (Mathematics Section Revised, 1970)

Piaget, Jean, et al. *The Child's Conception of Geometry.* New York: Basic Books Inc., 1960.

Swenson, Esther. *Making Primary Arithmetic Meaningful to Children.* Washington, D.C.: National Education Association, 1961.

X. EARLY EDUCATION AND PHYSICAL FITNESS

Anderson, Marion, et al. *Play with a Purpose.* New York: Harper & Row, Publishers, 1966.

Bucher, Charles, and Evelyn Reade. *Physical Education in the Modern Elementary School.* New York: The Macmillan Co., 1964.

Dauer, Victor. *Dynamic Physical Education for Elementary School Children.* Minneapolis: Burgess Publishing Co., 1968.

Duffy, Nona Keen, et al. *Can You Do This?* Elgin, Ill.: David C. Cook Publishing Co., 1954.

Farina, Albert, et al. *Growth Through Play*. Englewood Cliffs, N. J.: Prentice-Hall, 1963.

Kilander, H. Frederick. *School Health Education*. New York: The Macmillan Co., 1968.

Kirchner, Glenn. *Physical Education for Elementary School Children*. Dubuque, Iowa: Wm. C. Brown Co., 1966.

Moss, Bernice, W. H. Southworth, and J. L. Reichert, eds. *Health Education*. Washington, D. C.: National Education Association, 1961.

Nohl, Frederick, and Frederick Meyer, eds. *A Curriculum Guide for Lutheran Elementary Schools*. Vol. I. St. Louis: Concordia Publishing House, 1964. (Physical Education Section Revised, 1970)

Schurr, Evelyn. *Movement Experiences for Children*. New York: Appleton-Century-Crofts, 1967.

XI. PROFESSIONAL ORGANIZATIONS AND RESOURCE CENTERS PUBLISHING MAJOR WORKS IN EARLY CHILDHOOD EDUCATION

Association for Childhood Education International, 3615 Wisconsin Ave., N.W., Washington, D. C. 20016.

Publishes *Childhood Education* and bulletins pertaining to nursery schools, kindergarten, and elementary grades.

National Association for the Education of Young Children, 1629 21st Street, N.W., Washington, D. C. 20009.

Publishes *Young Children* and materials for early childhood education teachers.

National Education Association, 1201 16th Street, N.W., Washington, D. C. 20036.

The Department of Elementary-Kindergarten-Nursery Education publishes the newsletter *Early Education* and bulletins.

National Laboratory on Early Childhood Education, Dr. James O. Miller, Director, University of Illinois, 805 W. Pennsylvania Ave., Urbana, Ill. 61801.

Publishes a monthly newsletter, annotated bibliographies in the area of early childhood education, and research reports in early childhood development and education.

Office of Economic Opportunity, Washington, D. C.

Publishes materials and guides for head start programs.

Society for Research in Child Development, Inc., University of Chicago Press, 5750 Ellis Ave., Chicago, Ill. 60637.

Publishes *Child Development* quarterly; *Child Development Abstracts;* and *Child Development Monographs*.

U. S. Government Printing Office, Division of Public Documents, Washington, D. C. 20402.

Publishes a variety of materials concerned with current happenings in early childhood education.

INDEX